Praise for

"The Electoral College has been around since the founding of the United States yet is little understood by many people. In this book, Emily Conrad interviewed a number of electors to see why they did not follow their state's popular vote and what their actions tell us about this institution. It is a well-written account that brings the Electoral College to life and reveals the important role it plays in American politics."

—DARRELL WEST, Vice President and the
Douglas Dillon Chair in Governance Studies
at the Brookings Institution

"Assailed for violating the popular will, the faithless elector has generally been a rare bird. Not so in 2016, which produced both Democratic and Republican faithless, more than in any election in modern presidential history. Conrad got to know most of them, and the biographical narratives she shares are very revealing. Their reasons for violating pledges vary, but they appear public-spirited, not self-centered or authoritarian. Several of them assumed the label Hamilton electors, paying homage to the founder who most exposited elector free agency. Conrad's book has induced in me a reassessment of the character and motive of the 'faithless elector' even though I have taught the Electoral College since 1967."

—J. DAVID GILLESPIE, Ph.D., Dana Professor of
Political Science, Emeritus, Presbyterian College

"Emily Conrad's fascinating tales of 'faithless electors' are not merely about the Electoral College, but about how ordinary, politically engaged Americans are struggling to cope with the political turmoils of our time. That makes *The Faithless?* a particularly worthwhile read."

—BRADLEY A. SMITH, Josiah H. Blackmore II/Shirley M. Nault Professor of Law at Capital University Law School, former Federal Election Commissioner (2000–2005)

"Emily Conrad combines a rich historical perspective, together with first-hand accounts of faithless electors from the 2016 Presidential Election, to give the reader a real understanding of how the Electoral College actually functions."

—VAN D. HIPP, JR., Chairman of American Defense International, Inc.

"A fascinating look at one of the least understood aspects of our presidential electoral process. Conrad does an excellent job getting at the heart of the matter and addressing the major questions regarding the motives and intentions of faithless electors in a personal way. A refreshingly balanced perspective in a time of such political polarization."

—KENDRA STEWART, Professor of Political Science at the College of Charleston

"A well-written, approachable look into the most important part of our government that no one knows anything about."

—MARK LEMLEY, William H. Neukom Professor at Stanford Law School, Director of the Stanford Program in Law, Science, and Technology

"Emily Conrad provides *the* authoritative account of the extraordinary effort by presidential electors to deny Donald Trump the presidency through the formation of the 'Hamilton Elector' movement in 2016. While they were unsuccessful, a record number of so-called faithless electors emerged and their actions ultimately led to a Supreme Court battle over an elector's right to vote as they wish. In-depth interviews with key players make Conrad's work an invaluable resource for anyone looking to understand the inner-working of the 2016 Electoral College."

—ROBERT ALEXANDER, Founding Director of
Ohio Northern University's Institute for Civics and
Public Policy, author of *Representation and the Electoral College*
(Oxford University Press, 2019)

"Whether one is a scholar studying the peculiar workings of the United States Electoral College, or a citizen striving to understand its purpose and relevance in contemporary America, this book provides a unique and compelling perspective. As the author points out, our political system is undergoing increasing scrutiny from growing numbers of voters who realize that the dysfunction we are experiencing is systemic. Ms. Conrad's book adds new insights as she shares how a small group of serious and patriotic Americans interpreted their role as 2016 presidential electors within an important part of that system."

—DR. JIM REX, National Chairman of The Alliance Party,
former South Carolina State Superintendent
of Education (2007–2011)

"By discovering the thinking and motives of the so-called faithless electors who in 2016 tried to fix the broken, opaque, unfair, out-of-date process of the Electoral College system, this book reveals both why the American people are betrayed by this system of choosing the president and how individual citizens can take the responsibility for change. Emily Conrad has demystified the Electoral College and brought a needed sense of reality to the often arcane lawyerly debates about this otiose artifact of the 18th century. Because demographic change means that in this century the loser of the national popular vote routinely has a good chance to win the Electoral College, this book's call to reform should be heard."

—REED HUNDT, CEO and co-founder of
Making Every Vote Count, a nonprofit
dedicated to having every vote for president
matter equally, former Chairman of the
Federal Communications Commission (1993–1997)

"While most political junkies examined the unprecedented nature of Donald Trump's 2016 presidential victory, Conrad was fascinated by the underreported stories about the eight so-called faithless electors who cast ballots that went against the popular vote of their states in the Electoral College. The driving questions behind the author's work lie not in constitutional debates surrounding the legality of faithless electors or the undemocratic nature of the Electoral College, but in the eight electors themselves . . . her deeply human approach that centers on the personal lives of the eight electors is a welcome alternative to a genre dominated by hyperpartisan pundits. By pushing Trump and Clinton out of the spotlight, the book is also an implicit celebration of democracy with an unrelenting focus on state and local activists willing to stand up against members of their own parties." *—KIRKUS REVIEWS*

THE FAITHLESS?

THE FAITHLESS?

The Untold Story of the
Electoral College

EMILY CONRAD

Illustration credits
pp. xi, 11, 53, 89, 167: Graphics by Ryan Clark
p. 1: Images provided by Micheal Baca (top),
Bret Chiafalo (bottom)
p. 2: Images provided by Gage Skidmore (top),
Levi Guerra (middle), David Mulinix (bottom)
p. 3: Images provided by Robert Satiacum (top),
Art Sisneros (middle), Baoky Vu (bottom)

In memory of my mentor Patrick Caddell
and my Chilean host father Patricio Diaz Segovia,
both of whom passed away in 2019

Author's Note

I have written this book in accordance with the stories that my inter-
viewees presented to me. While some events, details, and dates may
not be factually accurate, I have chosen to write their stories in this way
to reflect how the electors have rationalized their experience with the
Electoral College. Some spectators on the ground of the 2016 caucuses,
state conventions, and elections may remember events differently.

Contents

Electoral College 101

ELECTORAL COLLEGE VOTES BY STATE

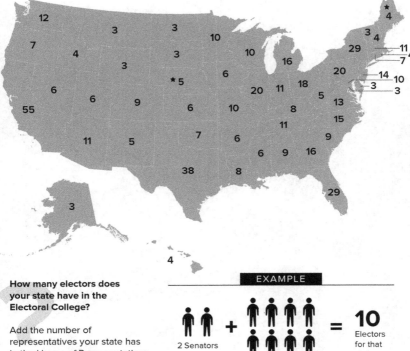

How many electors does your state have in the Electoral College?

Add the number of representatives your state has in the House of Representatives, with two (every state has two senators in the Senate).

EXAMPLE

2 Senators + 8 members of the House of Representatives = **10** Electors for that state

---

★ **2 states have adopted the "district congressional method"**

48 states and the District of Columbia are "winner-take-all" elections. If a candidate wins by even 0.01%, the candidate will receive all of that state's Electoral College votes.

Trump won an elector in Democrat **Maine** in 2016.

Obama won an elector in Republican **Nebraska** in 2008.

A candidate must have at least 270 of the 538 electoral votes* to become President.

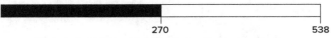

270   538

* If a majority of 270 is not reached, the President is chosen by the House of Representatives according to the 12th Amendment to the Constitution.

The Electors

MICHEAL BACA

State: Colorado; Party: Democratic

A former marine, Micheal was a 24-year-old graduate student, an Uber driver, and a Staples employee when chosen as an elector. He also co-founded the Hamilton Electors movement, an attempt to stop Donald Trump from taking office.

BRET CHIAFALO

State: Washington; Party: Democratic

A self-described nerd, Bret was able to monetize his passion for gaming computers. In 2016, when he became a co-founder of the Hamilton Electors, the 38-year-old was working at X-Box's command center. A long-time enthusiast of local politics, he had participated in every local caucus since he was 18.

BILL GREENE

State: Texas; Party: Republican

An ardent Ron Paul supporter, Bill stepped back from a career as a political consultant in Georgia in 2012 due to growing disillusionment with the Republican Party. He moved to Texas and decided to pursue a fresh start in academia as a political science professor at South Texas College.

LEVI GUERRA

State: Washington; Party: Democratic

Levi, a Hispanic woman from rural Washington state, came from an underprivileged home. When her dad lost his job, she worked during high school to help provide for her siblings. A mere eighteen years old, she was also a student at Big Bend Community College when chosen as an elector.

DAVID MULINIX

State: Hawaii; Party: Democratic

Originally from Ohio, David had long been a progressive activist since embracing the Native American warrior roots from his father. The 66-year-old was an independent voter tackling issues like Hawaii's homelessness and climate change before jumping on board the Bernie camp in 2015.

ROBERT SATIACUM

State: Washington; Party: Democratic

The son of a Puyallup chief, Robert only recently got involved in politics when he led a campaign to rename Mt. Rainier. The 56-year-old became disillusioned with politics at the 2016 Democratic National Convention and has since dedicated himself to environmental conservation.

ART SISNEROS

State: Texas; Party: Republican

Becoming a Christian transformed Art's life. Besides his normal job in industrial welding machinery, much of his time is taken up by home-schooling his six children. In 2016, he was active in the libertarian-leaning branch of the Republican Party and helped start a pro-life organization.

BAOKY VU

State: Georgia; Party: Republican

A former refugee from South Vietnam, Baoky was living out the American dream in Atlanta, working in the finance industry after having completed a MBA at Georgetown University. He got involved with the Republican Party in college, describing himself as a Reaganite and big-tent conservative.

Introduction

"One thing I want to make clear," 28-year-old Micheal Baca declares, "When I did what I did, I had no intention of overruling the will of the people. I was being faithful to the Constitution." His voice is impassioned, but not angry. Despite the fact that we are discussing politically polarizing topics, the former Marine and current high school government teacher approaches the conversation with a unique combination of confidence in his opinions and empathy for those who might disagree. "I understand when I am called a faithless elector; and I certainly understand your utilizing that phrase as you write. But I do not consider myself to be faithless."

Micheal is referring to that fateful day in mid-December 2016, when he acted as one of Colorado's nine electors of the Electoral College. He was

5

expected to follow precedent and cast his vote for the winner of Colorado's popular vote for President: Hillary Clinton. He didn't.

When fellow Colorado Democrats voted for Micheal to become a member of the Electoral College, it was March 2016, and he was still caucusing for Bernie Sanders. But he claims that it wasn't a dislike of Clinton or her policies that influenced his vote. He was most influenced by a handful of exit polls that showed that up to 25% of Republicans voted for Trump only because he was backed by the GOP, not because they agreed with his policies or his personality. "I thought that within the Electoral College, there was bound to be 37 Republicans who would not want to vote for Donald Trump, if they were given access to an alternative Republican candidate." So Micheal decided to follow a non-conventional, what he believed to be bipartisan, path: he voted for Republican Ohio governor John Kasich.

Micheal's focus on the number 37 is significant—if 37 Republican electors had decided to vote faithlessly in 2016, Trump would not have received the 270 Electoral College votes necessary to win. According to the Constitution, if a majority of Electoral College votes is not achieved, the President is decided within the House of Representatives. Would Trump have been able to emerge as the President, in this case? I have no answer to that question; however, I am tempted to rephrase conservative historian Niall Ferguson: history is not only about what happened, but also, about what didn't happen.

Indeed, nowhere near 37 Republican electors were faithless on the country's actual Election Day—not Tuesday, November 8, but Monday, December 19. Only two did. One of them was political science professor Bill Greene. "When I first put my name in the hat to become an elector at the Texas Republican State Convention, I didn't really think about who I was going to vote for," claims the fifty-four year old North Carolina native, in a boisterous voice that seems destined for the radio or the college classroom. Bill notes that during the May 2016 state convention, Trump's victory wasn't yet certain, and that there was still massive, grassroots support for the hometown wunderkind Republican Senator Ted Cruz.

"Once I received the electorship, however, I really got into the process; trying to understand how the writers of the Constitution intended the Electoral College to be run." Bill explains how in the months that followed, he pored over The Federalist Papers, James Madison's notes during the Constitutional Convention, and pronouncements from the Founding Fathers of the United States. "The more research I did, the more I respected the Founders as truly brilliant leaders with so much foresight. By December, I had resolved to vote my conscience for who I believed to be the highest qualified candidate." In Bill's mind, Donald Trump wasn't the most qualified candidate; Ron Paul was.

As I researched this book and talked with one faithless elector after another, I found myself constantly challenged in my ideas and understanding of the Electoral College, the role of political parties within America's democratic system, and the empowerment of the individual versus the masses in American politics. However, one thing that I do not question is the authenticity of the electors who decided to go against the popular votes of their states and vote faithlessly. Each one of the electors with whom I have spoken gave immense thought and emotional energy into his or her decision. They also viewed their role in the Electoral College as a great responsibility, one bestowed upon them by their peers and empowered by nothing less than the Constitution itself.

The individuals who either voted faithlessly or publicly considered a faithless vote included a Native American activist, a former refugee from Vietnam, a September 11th first responder, a Harvard-educated psychiatrist of African American and Native American descent, and a pro-life activist and homeschool father, among many others. Although they hailed from different socio-economic backgrounds and held different political and religious beliefs, they all decided to go against the mainstream, often to the ire of their respective political parties, as well as that of the general public.

Today, in America, there is a raging debate about whether the Electoral College should even exist. In writing this book, my intention is not to contribute to this debate, but rather to provide insights into how the Electoral College operates. In the 2016 election, the United States saw the most attempts to vote faithlessly in modern history. As political parties continue to decline in their appeal and power, the phenomenon of the independent voter continues to rise, and our culture continues to focus on the individual rather than the community, as evidenced by decreasing church and civic club memberships, I believe that faithless electors may become a more influential trend in future presidential election cycles. Rather than berate or praise faithless electors for their choices, understanding why they voted the way they did in 2016 enhances our understanding of the political future of the United States.

Considering that the presidential election of the United States is ultimately determined by 538 votes, I hope that this book encourages people to understand the Electoral College not only as it is enshrined in the Constitution, but also as it is practiced and institutionalized by each of the fifty states of the union, as well as the District of Columbia. "I always think it is kind of funny when I read things on the internet asking how a nineteen-year-old girl managed to become an elector and always allude to some sort of conspiracy theory," explains now active duty military Levi (or L.J.) Guerra, who was among the youngest of the 2016 electors.

One of the self-proclaimed "Hamilton Electors," an informal group of electors who were inspired by Alexander Hamilton's Federalist No. 68 to vote their conscience, L.J. threw her support behind four-star general Colin

Powell, who was Secretary of State under Republican President George W. Bush from 2001 to 2005, instead of Hillary Clinton. She remembered learning about the Electoral College in school, but didn't have a sense of how it worked, and no one seemed to be able to tell her. Figuring that the best way to learn was by experiencing the process firsthand, she decided to run as an elector. Her underprivileged background and eloquence beyond her years resonated with her fellow Washington Democrats. "The thing is, I know exactly how I became an elector; I know when I was chosen, and how, and by whom. And I recount my story to anyone," L.J. notes, then asks rhetorically. "Can most people say that? Do you know how your state chooses its electors?"

L.J.'s comment shines a light onto an important topic that is often forgotten when discussing the Electoral College. Sparse attention is given by mainstream media as to how the Electoral College, which is alarmingly decentralized with fifty-one different systems, is organized and implemented. While some states elect their electors at caucuses and conventions, other states have surprisingly undemocratic ways of choosing their electors. For example, in California's Democratic Party, each congressional and Senate nominee designates one elector. California's Republican electors are chosen directly by Republican state leadership, a widespread practice among many states. Meanwhile, Pennsylvania takes this to a new level, as Republican electors are handpicked directly by the Republican nominee for President and Democratic electors are handpicked by the Democratic one.

I hope that this book will encourage people to research and learn about how electors are chosen within their states, as well as prompt discussions about whether the Electoral College requires reform and standardization throughout the states. I would also like to present the idea that future discussions about the Electoral College might also include a national security component. The 2016 presidential election was rife with allegations of collusion and foreign interference, particularly through targeted advertising online. As there are only 538 votes in the Electoral College, and therefore only 538 individuals who have votes that truly count, it is possible for electors to be easily identified and targeted by bad-faith domestic or foreign actors.

Currently, 32 states and the District of Columbia have laws binding electors to the popular vote of their state, while 18 states do not. Among the states that do bind Electoral College votes, the cost of non-compliance is not necessarily substantial. Seventeen states and D.C. have no consequences for voting one's personal choice. In the case of Washington state, the four faithless electors of 2016 who did not vote for Hillary Clinton faced a fine of only $1,000, which is still being contested in federal court. Some argue that state laws that bind electors are inherently unconstitutional. At the time of writing, two cases originating from the 2016 election will be heard in the Supreme Court in May 2020 to determine the legality of party pledges and faithless electors in Colorado and Washington state. It is possible that the fate of the Electoral College system will be determined within America's court system, instead of by popular vote or Constitutional amendments.

2016 Electoral College

2016 ELECTION RESULTS
Electoral College Votes
270 VOTES TO WIN

Clinton/Kaine	Trump/Pence
227 Electoral College votes	**304** Electoral College votes

Popular Vote

65,853,516 votes	**62,984,825** votes

FAITHLESS VOTES

Validated

State	Presidential vote	VP vote	Name of Elector
HI	Bernie Sanders (D)	Elizabeth Warren (D)	David Mulinix
TX	John Kasich (R)	Carly Fiorina (R)	Christopher Suprun
	Ron Paul (R)	Mike Pence (R)	Bill Greene
WA	Colin Powell (R)	Maria Cantwell (D)	Levi Guerra
	Colin Powell (R)	Susan Collins (R)	Esther John
	Colin Powell (R)	Elizabeth Warren (D)	Bret Chiafalo
	Faith Spotted Eagle	Winona LaDuke	Robert Satiacum

Invalidated

State	Presidential vote	VP vote	Name of Elector
CO	John Kasich (R)	barred from voting	Micheal Baca
	Outcome: Replaced by alternate elector		
ME	Bernie Sanders (D)	Tim Kaine (D)	David Bright
	Outcome: During second vote, switched to Clinton		
MN	Bernie Sanders (D)	Tulsi Gabbard (D)	Muhammad Abdurrahman
	Outcome: Replaced by alternate elector		

Dropped Out Due to Personal Convictions

State	Name
GA	Baoky Vu
TX	Art Sisneros

Baoky Vu
Part 1

Baoky Vu still remembers the singular moment when he decided that he was going to be a Republican: it was when he was asked to play Ronald Reagan in a mock debate at his high school. For Baoky, it was a climactic moment. One of perhaps only ten Asian Americans in his high school of over 1,600 students in the suburban South, he had constantly been looking for ways to take on a leadership position there. Pushing himself outside of his comfort zone, he had run for student government, participated in the track team, and joined service clubs like Rotary Interact. All of his efforts were paying off: he was asked to play the leader of the free world.

This role took on special meaning for Baoky. His life had been turned upside down in 1975, when he fled Saigon with his mother and two younger brothers (one of whom was only 10 days old), some eight days

13

before South Vietnam fell to the North Vietnamese. His uncle, a USAID official, had arranged for the extended family to leave Saigon's Tan Son Nhat airport on a State Department C-130 flight. The following days were full of uncertainty and fear, as his family had no idea of the fate of his father, who had decided to stay to finalize some business before leaving. Baoky's small, broken family was shuffled from one location to another—from the Philippines to Guam to a makeshift Marine camp in southern California.

Although his description of these childhood experiences is surprisingly devoid of emotion, Baoky comments that it is difficult to recall happy moments, even when his family discovered that his father had miraculously been able to get out of Saigon via boat on the very day the city fell. Although the family was reunited, the anti-war sentiment in the United States proved to be too much for Baoky's father to handle emotionally. He moved the family to Australia, where he had studied in the 1960s, dedicating his time to increasing his professional credentials and getting additional support for the South Vietnamese cause. In 1977, the family decided to move back to the United States, when it was discovered that Baoky's grandmother (who had also been able to flee there) had developed lung cancer.

Baoky soberly comments that he was forced to attend five different elementary schools on three different continents between 1975 and 1977. He faced a myriad of cultural differences, including a language barrier. Prior to leaving South Vietnam, all of his formal schooling had been conducted in French and Vietnamese, which meant that his English was rudimentary. Ever an optimist with an infectious laugh, Baoky always tries to see the glass half full, though. "Being forced to move means that you have to learn how to adapt to different situations, or else you are at risk of completely losing your mind." He found an outlet in sports, because he discovered that he could bond more easily with others his age without having to worry about the language.

The family eventually landed in Atlanta, Georgia, where Baoky's father dedicated himself to academia, becoming a professor. His mother would eventually become an entrepreneur, opening Vietnamese pho noodle restaurants throughout the city with her sister and a group of friends. Moving to the suburbs in Gwinnett County, Baoky notes that they were one of the very few Asian American families in the area in the early 1980s.

Even now, Baoky laughs when he pictures himself playing Ronald Reagan in his school's debate. "Just imagine—a Vietnamese kid playing a former movie star and the President of the United States!" Baoky and one of his friends, who had been tasked with playing Walter Mondale, the Democratic opponent, did a lot of research to prepare for their roles. He remembers the 1984 election as the height of the Cold War, commenting that Russia had invaded Afghanistan five years earlier, but Reagan was standing firm against communism. Combing through the issues, Baoky found himself politically ignited, agreeing whole-heartedly with how Ronald Reagan approached foreign policy.

Perhaps with Baoky's family background and compelling refugee story, there was no choice but for him to get involved in politics. Growing up, both sides of his family had been politically active in Vietnam. His parents were in fact originally from North Vietnam, with standard Hanoi accents that they passed down to all three of their sons. In Saigon, Baoky's father was working for South Vietnam's National Army War College, researching why people defected from North Vietnam to South Vietnam. During their stint in Australia, Baoky remembers following his father around to political events, where his father would make anti-communist speeches.

His undergraduate studies solidified his identity as a Republican. Perhaps if Baoky had gone to a university in the Northeast or Pacific Coast, he would not have been swayed so much toward the Republican camp. But after high school, Baoky landed himself an Air Force ROTC scholarship and chose to study electrical engineering close to home at Georgia Tech University in Atlanta. He quickly realized, however, that the subject wasn't for him. It was too theoretical and cerebral, whereas Baoky enjoyed talking to people and making friends. He switched to studying both management and international affairs and found a new way to socialize: by joining the campus College Republicans.

Throughout the South, college campuses were organizing in support of the Republican Party. Baoky was drawn to the group because of what he now describes as the party's optimistic vision for the future. "I understand that this was also a product of the times," he comments. "You were witnessing the defeat of communism around the world. Republicans were standing up for opening up the world and reducing barriers. They wanted free trade and globalization." As he pictured what that looked like, Baoky thought that this was the sort of future in which he could succeed and thrive.

After graduating, Baoky was drawn to the nation's capital and political mecca, Washington, D.C. He applied for the Master of Business Administration program at Georgetown University, and was accepted. In Washington, Baoky felt like he had discovered where he belonged. His political ideas and beliefs matured as he met people from all over the country, noting that he was taking classes alongside Nancy Pelosi's son, Paul. Taught by legendary figures like the former U.N. Ambassador Jeane Kirkpatrick, he began to think about what it really meant to be a conservative. Over time, he found himself taking a more nuanced stance on the issues, rather than seeing everything as black-or-white. "You think about Edmund Burke, who is widely viewed as the father of the conservative movement. He said—and I quote—'change is the means of our preservation,'" Baoky tells me as he discusses his own political beliefs. "My thought on conservatism is that we should have self-restraining mechanisms as we progress. But that doesn't mean that we shouldn't progress."

When asked about how he developed this pragmatic understanding, Baoky doesn't attribute it to the adaptability that he developed while growing up on three different continents, but rather to having grown up within a multi-faith household. Although Baoky learned the tenants of Christianity through his father's Catholic family, his mother was a Buddhist. As he grew older and thought back on his childhood, he was inspired by his mother's pragmatism. She read the Bible carefully, not so that she could adopt the faith for herself, but so that she could adopt some of its principles in her own life. Looking back, he sometimes thinks that these were the fundamental experiences that would later set him apart from his fellow Georgian Republicans. His upbringing made him respect and consider other people, even if they had different religious or political beliefs.

"We have to adapt to the times," Baoky comments. "Just as we are no longer the same people that we were twenty or thirty years ago, our country has changed." At Georgetown, Baoky flirted with the idea of going into the policy arena himself, taking advantage of all the lectures and resources at Georgetown to better understand foreign policy as the Cold War came to an end. He began to take what he describes as a more pragmatic view of a struggle that had previously defined his entire life—the fight against communism. "During my Georgetown days, I became less ideological against communism. I am a firm believer that constructive engagement can do a lot better than isolationism. Just as the United States changes, communist countries can also change and adapt with the right pressure and circumstances."

Although a part of Baoky desperately wanted to stay in Washington to begin a career in public policy, he felt a strong pull to return to Atlanta. In

1991, his mother began chemotherapy for lymphoma. Both of his brothers were otherwise engaged—one stationed in Hawaii, serving a five-year term in the Navy, and the other beginning medical school—and couldn't be there to help his parents. Baoky loved D.C., and even now remembers his time at Georgetown as the "best two years of [his] life." At the same time, he knew that politics often intersected with business, and that he would have the opportunity to jump into the political game later in life. He returned to Atlanta and joined the investment world.

It was a decision that he would not regret. After a relatively long career, he married a lawyer and had two children. They settled in Decatur, Georgia, where Baoky notes that he and his wife are clearly in the minority: he estimates that 85% of Decatur residents are Democrats, and the rest are Republicans. When I ask him how he likes to spend his free time, he laughs and comments, "Coaching Little League twice a week does not leave much time for anything else. Nor does walking the dogs three times a day." Now fifty-two years old, much of his life revolves around his elementary school and middle school children. He is happy that his parents live only about 10 miles away, in part because it means that his children are growing up speaking Vietnamese with their grandparents, so the language and culture are being passed down from one generation to another in a natural way.

If he does have time, Baoky likes to read books, play golf, go running, or watch ESPN or James Bond movies. Even though Baoky has remained in the business world, politics has continued to be an integral and time-consuming part of his life. After returning to Atlanta, Baoky discovered that he was a very persuasive fundraiser for both local and national Republican candidates.

Baoky's fundraising opened the door to the policy arena that he so wanted to be a part of during his days at Georgetown. During George W.

Bush's administration, he was given a political appointment on the Presidential Advisory Commission for Asian American and Pacific Islanders, which was housed under the Department of Health and Human Services. Every six weeks to two months, he traveled to meet with a variety of stakeholders—from business owners to healthcare service providers—to learn about the challenges they faced as members of the Asian community. For Baoky, this was extremely enlightening, as he began to think about the access to and engagement of Asian Americans with the government.

Baoky began to realize that as one of the few Vietnamese in politics, he was unique. It didn't hurt that he appreciated and supported the Republican establishment. Baoky comments on how different the George W. Bush administration was compared to the Trump administration: "George W. did a good job. One thing that he didn't mind doing was hiring smart people to work for him. Think of the people in his administration from Colin Powell to Hank Paulson. Each person had their own set of values. They were not folks who were sycophants; nothing like this cult of personality nowadays." When prodded, Baoky proudly lists the names of high-level Republicans he has had the opportunity to meet, including Senator Mitt Romney and the late John McCain, saying that it was "an honor" to help them with their Georgia campaigns.

"I was used to that type of Republican," Baoky admits later, when discussing the growing unease with the direction of the Republican Party that he was already starting to feel back in 2009. "I saw all of these stories about Barack Obama being born in Kenya or about his aiding Muslim extremism. The whole thing was frightening. Stories kept popping up, but it was clearly fake news." Focusing on pragmatism, Baoky believed that the ability to reach across the aisle was important—and he felt like the Georgia Republican Party was becoming too extreme for his liking. "I am open-minded about social issues," he remarks, "Most of my political beliefs have to do with international and fiscal issues. And right now, government spending is completely out of control."

Baoky began to see the Republican Party changing, especially as the Tea Party movement took off. As they worked together under the party umbrella, Baoky added them as friends on his social media, but was in disbelief about the things that they were sharing, especially regarding religious fundamentalism. He felt like the positive vibes of the Reagan era were being overshadowed by anger and resentment, coupled with a lack of feasible solutions. "I mean, praying for rain isn't going to help when our climate is changing!" he exclaims.

In spite of some of the recent changes in the Republican Party, by the time 2016 had rolled around, Baoky wasn't extremely concerned. He continued to serve on state boards for Georgia Governor Nathan Deal, and felt like the establishment Republicans had persevered. "For a while, a lot of intelligent people were concerned by the rise of the Ron Paul and Rand Paul supporters. It wasn't so much their ideas, but that they had a tendency to come and go. They never really got involved. They didn't make any plans. Basically, they just made a lot of noise at the local conventions." As he looked at the roster of Republican candidates, from Jeb Bush to Marco Rubio to John Kasich, Baoky was sure that the Republicans had a good shot at the White House.

Levi Guerra
Part 1

"I was only eighteen years old when I was elected to the Electoral College," the now 23-year-old Levi Guerra comments. "When I think back on it, I realize how in the dark I was. I wasn't really educated about the Electoral College. I knew what it was from school, but I didn't understand how it worked." During our first conversation, Levi (who now goes by L.J., War, or Guerra) is quick to point out her motivation in talking to me: she wants to inspire individuals to start looking into the Electoral College and researching it. Describing it as a "big gray area" in the United States political system, she truly believes that more attention will ensure that the Electoral College does not remain nebulous.

Besides outlining her involvement in the 2016 Electoral College, L.J. is careful to steer away from most political or partisan questions. I quickly adapt and quit asking them, and our conversations about her experience in the Electoral College flourish. Almost immediately after casting her Electoral College vote, L.J. started looking to join the military. Nearly one year to the day after the vote, on December 11, 2017, she was shipped out for boot camp. Due to her service in the military, L.J. tries to remain completely apolitical—that is, as apolitical as she can, considering that she is part of a Supreme Court case that will likely have a long-term impact on all presidential elections for decades to come. She emphasizes that her political beliefs are her own and are not a representation of the military.

L.J. makes a surprisingly mature comment on politics for her age, based on the people she encountered in her very brief career in the political spotlight: "I know that when it comes to politics, you can really get into your own head. You let the issue overwhelm you until it gets to the point that it becomes the only thing you can feel and the only thing you can think. I don't want that to be my life."

The Electoral College only comes up rarely in L.J.'s new life in the military. Sometimes, she will joke with new friends, telling them not to Google her name (which lands more than 19 million results). When they inevitably do, she might tell them about her experience as an elector. But according to her, most of her friends don't really get it: they just respond with a, "Wow, that's cool."

She isn't turned off by their seeming disinterest or lack of understanding; it is what she has come to expect. When she was chosen as an elector and rushed home to tell her parents, their reaction also left a lot to be desired. "They didn't quite understand what being an elector meant," L.J. now laughs. "Sure, they were proud of me. But, they were more proud of me in the way like, 'Wow, that is great. We are happy that you are out there, keeping yourself busy, and doing this . . . thing.'"

L.J. was raised in what she describes as a relatively apolitical, broken family in rural Washington state. She lived with her biological father until she was fifteen years old, after which she was disowned for dating someone that he didn't approve of. "I come from a very Hispanic family background, who have very conservative traditions," she comments, describing her decision to move in with her mother and her stepfather (whom she refers to as "my father" throughout our conversations). It was a big transition for L.J.—while her biological father was fairly well-off financially, her mother and her father were not. Her father supported her mother and the entire family of six children with his Marine Corps sergeant's salary. That all changed in 2012, according to L.J., when a new policy put a cap on how long someone could stay in the same position before getting pushed out. Because of his lack of education, her father found himself without advancement potential and later, without a job. It was the beginning of financial hardship for the family.

"My parents were interested in elections and their outcomes; but they didn't encourage us to be involved," L.J. comments. "They just told us that we needed to make sure that we went out and voted." Indeed, L.J. kind of stumbled into political life. She recalls that she had been through a bad breakup and that she was wallowing in self-pity. As she was scrolling through Facebook, reading her friends' comments, she had an epiphany: the best way to snap out of this was to get involved in something bigger than herself. Elections were coming up, and she thought that would be a good outlet for her. She resolved to put everything she could into politics.

L.J. felt like she leaned slightly more toward the left than toward the right, but she was more interested in getting involved in local politics than in national or presidential politics. She felt like a lot of the dialogue centering around national politics didn't really pertain to her or her community. Yes, she grew up a second-generation American in a Hispanic household, but her experiences in rural Washington were different from those of Hispanics in large cities. While her parents spoke Spanish to her in the home, they encouraged her to respond to them in English. She picked up proper Spanish only after she started taking Spanish classes in high school, although she remembers trips down to Mexico to the state of Nuevo Leon, where she would meet up with her mother's family. (That all ended when her mother divorced her biological father and, like L.J., ended up disowned by her family.)

"I was researching politics all of the time and was getting a sense of how the system worked," L.J. comments. The focus on local politics meant that she was going to start at the lowest level of Washington's caucus system. She tried to attend at least one political event or meeting each week. "I have heard that a lot of being involved in politics is just actually showing up. I think that it was definitely my case. People got so used to seeing me at events, that I kept moving up the caucus system." Of course, L.J. kept putting her name in the hat; she viewed this as a learning experience.

As a high school student, she had already started taking classes at Big Bend Community College, where she had decided that she was going to pursue her associate degree. It was a thirty-minute drive from home, but she enjoyed learning at a higher academic level. Besides being a student, she was working as a teacher's assistant. Once she graduated in June 2016, she began any job that she could pick up. Her favorite job was a provider of assistance and companionship to people with disabilities, which she recalls as personally fulfilling. It was a role that came naturally to her, as she had an aunt with Down syndrome and a younger sister with autism. Leaving that job to go into the military was a challenging personal transition for L.J., who noted that she cried over having to leave some of her clients.

In spite of L.J.'s difficult youth, she doesn't dramatize her experience, but rather talks about it in a matter-of-fact way, making her quiet strength and determination to make the most of her life all the more impressive.

When I ask whether she views herself as an optimist, a pessimist, or something in between, she calmly replies, "I have always come to expect the worst in any situation. I think that I am getting a healthier perspective. In the military, we are taught to expect the worst, but to hope for the best. Besides, I get a paycheck twice a month and I have a roof over my head and enough to eat. When I was younger, I couldn't count on this, and I think that made me kind of pessimistic."

At one point, as a high school student, L.J. was the only one in her family of eight who was working. She gave up most of the money that she earned to help provide for the family. "It was such a tough time for my family that I don't remember the time frame," she comments. "Was it one month? Two months? I cannot remember; I wasn't thinking about the time frame when it was happening. We lost the home that we were living in because we couldn't afford it. Our cars got repossessed. It was really bad, but somehow my mother managed to find a job." Even though she calls herself a pessimist, she comments that her family has persevered through tough times, which have made them even stronger and brought them closer together—the proverbial silver lining to a dark cloud. "I love my parents dearly and I know that they always did their best."

These experiences may have made L.J. think that it would be better to caucus for Bernie Sanders than for Hillary Clinton. But this is speculation, as L.J. carefully avoids sharing her political viewpoints in our conversations. She simply notes, "I thought that Sanders might better represent me as an individual, rather than Clinton." She enjoyed moving up through the ranks of the caucus system, not only because it satisfied her intellectual curiosity and gave her a new outlet, but also because she got to make new friends. On the day of the Congressional Caucus, she was taking the three-hour drive down to Seattle with one of her classmates from Big Bend Community College, who had also worked her way up the caucus system. They had another friend who had advanced past the county level caucus, but intentionally skipped the Congressional Caucus. Once it became evident that Bernie wasn't going to win Washington, he thought that it wasn't worth spending the time to caucus anymore. L.J. was more pragmatic about the whole thing; she was going in part to learn.

Already, L.J. was quite proud of herself. She had just gotten involved in politics and was only one of two people who had been selected to represent her hometown at the Congressional Caucus. She estimates that there were only about ten people from her native Grant County. When she arrived to the Congressional Caucus, she saw that there was a sign-up sheet for people trying to be electors. There were already about sixty people signed up, but L.J. decided that she would also give it a go. "Anyone could sign up at that point to become an elector, but not just anyone made it to the caucus," she comments. "I think that overall, there were three previous caucus elections that allowed me to eventually represent my voting region at the Congressional Caucus. I wasn't there by accident."

She is referring to the comments that would eventually proliferate online about her becoming an elector in the Electoral College; many of them alluding to some sort of non-existent conspiracy. "When I went up to the table, I had no idea how it worked. They told me to put down my name and that I needed to make a one-minute speech at the end of the day. Then we would vote to see who would be the elector," she remembers. Deciding that she wanted to learn more about how the Electoral College worked, she threw her hat in the ring. If she didn't get it, it would be fine—at least she would learn something in the process.

The thought of making yet another speech was something that scared her. She claims that her stint in the military has bestowed upon her a newfound confidence in expressing her ideas and opinions. She proudly states that she has even been recently asked to say prayers publicly, with many of her friends affectionately calling her "Preacher Guerra." As a practicing Catholic, she always wears the saints around her neck, even if she doesn't go to mass as frequently as she would like.

At the time, though, she claims that she was nearly paralyzed with stage fright when she was asked to do public speaking. She knew that she would need to prepare a speech beforehand rather than ad-libbing something. She walked outside to get away from the commotion and sat down. "I thought about the type of person I was; what made me different. I thought about the people who I would represent," she comments, "I thought about my community. I jotted down some basic ideas on a piece of paper and then went inside." During the lunch break, she went back outside to practice.

When it came time for her to give her speech, she stood up before all of the members of the Congressional Caucus. She was still nervous, but when she opened her mouth, the words just began to flow. "I can be a very passionate person sometimes. I can also be a pretty angry person, if I allow myself to go there. When I started speaking, all of this started coming out and I think that some people really liked what I was saying," she comments. L.J. focused on talking about her constituency and her desire to represent her community in the Electoral College. "I said something along the lines that everyone likes to talk about the individuals of color from less fortunate backgrounds: the young, rural Hispanics. I told them that I was there to represent that part of Washington. I was there to represent the youth."

L.J. didn't expect to win. Even so, she wasn't the youngest person who tried to become an elector that day. She saw that there were a few people who were quite polished from a political perspective, recalling one man who was slightly older than her and gave what she describes as almost a professional speech. When her name was called as the winner, she was surprised.

While many of the people at the Congressional Caucus were primarily interested in becoming a delegate to the Democratic National Convention. L.J. didn't even seriously consider the option. "The thing is, the only ones who can actually end up going to the DNC are the ones who are good at fundraising or already well-off enough that they can pay their own way. I didn't even have a stable home; there was no way that I was going to pay to go to the DNC." Indeed, she later comments, one of the reasons that she ran for the Electoral College to begin with was that it was free to participate in.

When she went back home to her friends and family, their reactions about her becoming an elector were anticlimactic to say the least. She describes it as if it just didn't click in their brains. Although she beat out some sixty people to become an elector, she began to not think of it as a very big deal either, until one day she casually mentioned it to one of her school friends. "He was so surprised, saying, 'Holy cow, your vote is actually one of the ones that really matters.'" As she began to think about it, she realized that it was true; her becoming an elector was a very important thing and, true to herself, she began to research more about it.

Bill Greene
Part 1

2012 was a watershed moment for Bill Greene: it was the year that he decided that he would leave all the partisan politics behind him and start a new life and career as a political science professor at South Texas College in Weslaco. "I saw the very worst side of politics when I became involved in Ron Paul's campaign; especially of party politics," remembers Bill, still with a hint of sadness in his voice, recalling former colleagues and friends who became "straight out nasty" during the Republican primary, which was ultimately won by former Massachusetts governor Mitt Romney.

For the former co-chair of Ron Paul's campaign in the state of Georgia, the impetus for Bill's career change was not personal slights, but rather the systemic failures of the Republican Party itself. "I watched as these Republicans in leadership reacted to the young people coming into the party through Ron Paul; they just essentially slapped them down," Bill exclaims. "It is exactly what the Democrats did to the young people attracted by Bernie Sanders in 2016. They told them that there was no place for them in the Democratic Party."

Throughout our conversations, Bill has few traces of the partisanship which defined his prolific decades-long career in political consulting and activism. Instead, picturing himself as a lone conservative in a sea of liberals and contributing to "campus viewpoint diversity," Bill has accepted his new role in academia by encouraging intellectual curiosity in his students, most of whom he claims fall left of center. The way in which he discusses politics is thoughtful. This appears to be a change for a man who was formerly advertised as a "rising star in politics" and a "conservative internet guru."

"When it comes to political figures, the one thing that I admire the most is consistency. I admire people who don't sell out their beliefs, just because it will give them short-term bonus points. And I don't give a crap about political parties. I think that parties can be useful tools to advance an agenda, but, to be honest, neither of the two major political parties now has a clue." Bill easily rambles off lists of Republicans he admires, like Thomas Massie [Republican Congressman from Kentucky], Justin Amash [Independent Congressman from Michigan], Rand Paul [Republican Senator from Kentucky], and Mike Lee [Republican Senator from Utah].

But when asked about Democratic political figures, Bill doesn't miss a beat—Bernie Sanders's consistency is enough to warrant Bill's respect, even if his policies aren't. Bill sees Bernie Sanders and Ron Paul as cut from the same cloth, fighting the same fight election cycle after election cycle, their sincerity winning over voters in an increasingly jaded political atmosphere. "I also appreciate Tulsi Gabbard [the Democrat Congresswoman from Hawaii]; even though I completely disagree with her political ideas," Bill notes. "You cannot help but admire her. She is willing to buck her own party line. And it isn't to advance her own cause, because it often comes at the expense of herself."

While seemingly a sharp change, Bill's break from active political involvement did not come from out-of-the-blue; it was a slow realization of the inherent apathy within the political system. "While I worked as a political consultant, I met with lots and lots of politicos and even more candidates. And as you meet more and more of these types of people, you become more jaded and cynical, because you realize that so many of these people are only in politics for the power or the money. They are not making the changes that this country needs." When given a chance to leave his career, Bill took it without much of a second thought.

Academia might always have been a more natural place for Bill, who grew up in a family of teachers in the picturesque mountains of western North Carolina, in a small hamlet called Etowah. "If you aren't looking for it," laughs Bill, "Chances are that you are going to miss it." Today, Etowah has less than 7,000 residents, and, while it lacks the ubiquitous Wal-Mart, it is home to a small library, an elementary school, a supermarket, and a Dollar General.

Bill's father was a college professor who later transitioned to computer programming. His mother and stepfather were public school teachers. "Every day at the dinner table, I would hear all of their stories and I swore to myself that I would never become a teacher like them." That all changed when Bill started studying for his associate degree at the nearby Brevard College, later transferring to study political science at the University of North Carolina at Asheville. "I discovered that I really loved studying and began to think about continuing my education and becoming a teacher myself, but at the college level or above."

Throughout his multi-faceted career, Bill always made time for adjunct teaching at local universities and colleges, utilizing his master's in political science from the University of North Carolina at Greensboro and PhD coursework in international relations at Florida International University. And so, in 2013, Bill settled relatively seamlessly into the life of a professor in Texas, eventually finding a new romance, remarrying, and getting two dogs, Ellie and Cato. To increase his career credentials, he picked up writing his PhD dissertation at the University of Leicester and started boosting his publication count and academic conference attendance.

Bill also started compiling a bucket list and slowly began to check items off it. For a while, he spent weekends taking scuba classes to get his scuba certification. Once he started, however, he realized that his bucket list had a major kink: it didn't take into account that he had a problem with seasickness; which relegated him to going to scuba in deep lakes in Texas, rather than the ocean. "I am just a typical, middle-class college professor," Bill claims. "Most of my spare time is spent reading. I think that I am kind of average. I am worried about what a lot of other people my age worry about: Will I be able to retire?"

For Bill, however, this question isn't based on his financial acumen or foresight. It all comes down to politics: "Normal people like us; we ultimately don't have much power over this. With foreign exchange controls, the dollar could depreciate very easily, making it next to impossible for people my age to retire. Will the real value of the dollar remain valuable? And besides that, will Social Security even be able to last that long?"

In spite of Bill's ability and willingness to at least consider the other side of the aisle, his retirement worries underscore the intensity of his strong political beliefs. The self-proclaimed libertarian comes across almost as a single-issue voter: solving America's "crushing" national debt problem. "How can it be that the debt consistently goes up one trillion dollars and then another trillion dollars and another trillion dollars and absolutely no one mentions it? It is just insane. And the thing is, you cannot blame one party or another in this situation; this is a bipartisan effort to keep raising our debt ceiling. I think if it is not resolved, it will crash the economy," Bill passionately asserts.

Once he is on the topic, words keep rolling out of his mouth before he apologizes for having gone on a tangent. Still, he envisions an alternate future of government interventionism due to economic downturn and increased possibilities for "tyranny to take hold." Borrowing the quint-essential phrase from Ron Paul's 2009 book, Bill's solution is to "end the Fed" (in simple terminology), or to transition to a free market economy with free market monetary policy without the involvement of the Federal Reserve (in more academic terms.)

Like most professors who believe passionately in a political or social issue, Bill cannot help but bring up the national debt in his Introduction to American Politics classes, noting that most of his students have a hard time fathoming the number. "They get upset, and rightly so, asking, 'Why is no one telling us about this?'" Bill is worried about many of his students, saying that massive student loans "have almost completely ruined the higher education system." Although he likes to think of himself as an optimist (after all, "in the history of mankind's existence, our lives just keep getting better and better"), he admits that he is a bit of a pessimist in the short-term, sharing his belief that the current generation of young people could very quickly become worse-off than their parents' generation. "If this happens, if the national debt blows up, the young people will blame us—the older generations, their parents and their grandparents—for not doing anything about it. And, of course, they will be right."

With such passionate beliefs, Bill found that it was easier to maintain two Facebook profiles: one in which he can share conservative memes with friends and colleagues from his former life, without the possibility of reproach, and one to engage and debate with current (more liberal) colleagues, to help contribute to mutual understanding across the aisle.

With the 2016 election nearing, Bill's Facebook feeds took an unusual and interest-piquing turn; providing insights into the intrigue of both parties during the primary races. When Trump announced his candidacy on the Trump Tower escalators in New York City, Bill couldn't help but just laugh. "I thought that Trump was going to add some interesting aspects and ideas into the election cycle, especially inside the Republican Party; but I thought he had no chance at winning." As things progressed, Bill began to think that politics was "making no sense anymore." Normally he liked to offer predictions and ideas for his students and colleagues to consider, but Bill said that he couldn't do it in 2016. "When people would ask, I told them that four, eight, or sixteen years ago, I would have had lots of ideas and opinions to share. But with this election, I just couldn't tell anymore."

Although he had sworn not to get involved in politics after 2012 so as to focus all of his efforts on teaching, Bill found himself drawn to what was turning out to be an historic election year. "I told myself that I didn't have to get back into that hyper-partisan stuff; I didn't have to join in the tribalistic camps that are modern-day political parties."

It was clearly a struggle for Bill, who years later still describes weighing the pros and cons of involvement with intensity. "For a while, I kept telling myself: 'Bill, you are not from here. You don't have skin in the game in Texas. Just focus on bringing your political experience into the classroom. Stay focused. Teach your students. Don't get involved in local politics.'" Eventually, it was the classroom that helped him make up his mind: Bill convinced himself that he would become a much better teacher of the Electoral College system if he became an elector himself. Noting that a lot of his students had a tough time picturing the nameless 538 electors who determine the President every four years, he thought the Electoral College might come more alive if they could put a name and face to the process.

However, the fateful thing that sent Bill over the edge was his bucket list. "In my life, I had already been a delegate to the Republican National Convention; but I had never been an elector in the Electoral College before," says Bill. "And now that I hit my 50s, I began to think realistically, how many presidential election cycles do I actually have left?"

Perhaps Bill's bucket list dream of becoming an elector was influenced by his early mentor and Electoral College scholar, Roger MacBride. Roger had hosted a campaign fundraiser for Bill at his house in Miami, in a failed bid at the Florida State House after moving there to be closer to his wife's family. Bill still notes with pride that his campaign was the first time that Roger's Liberty Caucus PAC had supported a Republican candidate for the Florida State House.

It marked a transition for MacBride, who was previously a major player in the Libertarian Party (including a 1976 presidential candidate), as he moved back to the Republican Party. While MacBride might be most well-known to the American public for his behind-the-scenes role as a producer for *The Little House on the Prairie* from 1974 to 1983, he had an additional claim to fame in political circles: not voting for Richard Nixon as a Republican elector in the 1972 election. In so doing, Roger became one of the nation's most conspicuous faithless electors.

By the way that Bill talks, it is clear that he has nothing but respect for Roger MacBride, which makes it difficult to ascertain what sort of effect Roger had on Bill's Electoral College tenure. Did Bill have the express intent to vote for Ron Paul, instead of the actual Republican candidate, when he first expressed interest in running as a Texas elector? Bill certainly knew that electors were free agents from his friendship with Roger McBride. However, Bill claims that he wasn't thinking about who he would vote for when he put his name in the hat; he claims that he was thinking about his bucket list.

Besides, Bill knew that the Texas Republicans had already hand-picked their favorites to be the electors. Although electors are determined by public vote at the Texas Republican Convention, Bill knew that he was facing an uphill battle. "I knew there was a big chance that I wasn't going to get it," Bill says. "But I had to give it a shot."

Micheal Baca
Part 1

"The current generation is worse off than the previous one. The cost of living just keeps on increasing and wages have not been able to catch up," Micheal Baca comments soberly. "It is getting harder and harder for us just to get by. The younger generation is now relying on the 'gig economy' to pay the bills, not just for the extra income."

The now 28-year-old public high school government teacher in Las Vegas, Nevada, should know—when he was a Colorado elector in the 2016 election, he was only making ends meet through his gigs as an Uber driver and as a Staples employee, even though he had just finished a Master in Education with an emphasis in Human Relations from Northern Arizona University. "My situation is getting better now," he asserts, with a surprisingly refreshing optimism that infuses most of our conversations. "In comparison to other people my age, especially those who didn't finish school, I am doing pretty good. Previously, I was seriously just scraping by. But now I can say that I am a member of the lower-middle class. There is stability in my life, and finally, I can say that I am pretty excited for the future."

That sentiment has been a long time coming for Micheal, whose young adult life was beset by tragedy following his mother's suicide in 2013. At the time, he was a weather forecaster for the Marine Corps, stationed at the Keesler Air Force Base in Biloxi, Mississippi, something akin to what he describes as a dream job (he later called his stint in the Marines one of "the proudest things [he had] ever done.") He had joined to show his support for the United States after a one-year stint in England infused him with renewed appreciation for his country.

Unfortunately, his mother's suicide triggered his own depression, a struggle he admits that he deals with daily. After almost two years in the service, Micheal felt like he could no longer continue, and was honorably discharged in 2014 for hardship reasons. "I did the very best I could do," he reminisces, "but it is my greatest professional failure that I was unable to stick it out in the Marines."

He immediately returned to his 28,000-person hometown of Kingman, Arizona, to start grappling with the past head-on. In our conversations, he returns time and again to the topic of his mother's suicide—from how it influenced his opinions on gun control ("she still would have found a way to take her own life, but even so, all guns should be required to be both registered and insured") to how he built a memorial for her and planted a tree in her memory (which he counts among his greatest personal accomplishments, alongside his recent weight loss.) However, a few months later, when his then-girlfriend suggested a move to Denver, Micheal was ready for a change of scenery.

They arrived in their newly adopted city in June 2014, right before the midterms. "But I really didn't have much of a concept about the importance of midterm elections," Michael hesitates, but his honest and confessional nature gets the better of him. "I hate to admit this, but I didn't have the best voting record before 2016. I voted in the 2012 presidential election for Barack Obama, but that was about all."

Perhaps Micheal's relative political apathy was influenced by his upbringing, which he describes as an apolitical Hispanic household that leaned left from time to time. "My family is of Mexican descent, but we didn't cross the border; the border crossed us at some point. My father's family was originally from northern New Mexico and southern Colorado. I never knew my mother's family, but I took a DNA test and I suspect that's where my pale skin comes from," he says. Although he grew up culturally Hispanic, his family only spoke English in the home, something which Micheal has sought to rectify by learning basic conversational Spanish, which he puts to use during occasional trips to Mexico.

"I always had a political nature, though," Micheal notes. "I don't think it would surprise people who knew me that I would become an elector and do something like this." However, Micheal's political activism was almost cut prematurely short in 2008, when he was sixteen years old. He had volunteered at a phonebank for Hillary Clinton's Democratic primary run, an experience that left him completely "petrified" and turned him off politics for the next several years.

"It wasn't like I was completely ignorant, though," he claims. "I knew who the President and Vice-President and the major players in government were. And I kept up with the news. I just wasn't politically engaged." Sometimes, he donated money to campaigns or candidates he liked, but it was always part of some larger fundraising campaign that candidates had to boost their numbers of grassroots supporters. "It might be something like, 'Give us $3 and we will give you a sticker.' That was as much as I could afford. Basically, it was my way of saying, 'Yes, I am here and appreciate what you are doing.'"

That all changed in 2015, when Micheal attended Bernie Sanders's rally at the University of Denver. The turnout was so large that the overflow spilled past the gymnasium into a nearby lacrosse field, which streamed Sanders's speech via its scoreboard. With some media outlets estimating the turnout as more than 5,000 people, it was a sign that Hillary Clinton would face a surprisingly competitive challenger, with *Washington Post* reporter John Wagner claiming "the extraordinary turnout was the latest evidence that Sanders, 73, has tapped into the economic anxiety of the Democratic electorate."

"I wanted to volunteer right away," Micheal remembers. He even visited a Sanders field office later in the campaign cycle to find ways to help. Sanders's focus on tackling rising wealth inequality likely resonated deeply with Micheal, who seems to distrust most established financial institutions. Still angry about the 2008 financial crisis, he claims "people in every capital city in every state should still be protesting what Wall Street did to us." However, his distrust isn't limited to Wall Street, but extends to the government players he believes support their agenda, including the Federal Reserve, which he believes should be audited and investigated.

The 115th Congress, elected alongside Trump in the 2016 election, lost his trust after they provided tax benefits to the already wealthy. "Not that the 116th Congress is doing much better," he adds. "Even with Democratic control in 2018, it really hasn't gotten any better. Maybe a little, but not that much more than that." When asked what grade he would give Congress, he laughs, saying that in his classroom he is a notoriously easy grader. "If a kid shows up and writes their name on a paper, I give them 50% just for that. I think that my grade for Congress is also somewhere in that ballpark."

Today, he notes that his ideal political platform would be a mix between Bernie Sanders and 2016 Democratic presidential primary candidate/businessman Andrew Yang. He believes that Yang's focus on universal basic income could solve a lot of problems in the country, saying, "income inequality and wealth inequality cannot be solved by increasing the minimum wage or by more welfare benefits." Most of Micheal's ideas lean toward the progressive side of the Democratic Party. He forgoes moderate figures like former Vice President Joe Biden for legendary figures like Reverend Jesse Jackson or fiery social justice warriors like Kamala Harris [the Senator from California].

Perhaps unsurprisingly, he has a difficult time seeing eye-to-eye with the Republican Party, in part for its inability to address what he believes to be the most pressing issue facing both the country and the world today: climate change. "I don't want to quantify people's suffering by saying that one issue is more important than the other," he explains. "But one thing is for sure—climate change affects every single living being on the planet. Our inability to address this issue will already have massive repercussions."

After a relatively short conversation about his political beliefs and priorities, Micheal quickly pulls the plug, changing the topic to something he claims is much more important than tough political leadership—working across the aisle to get things done. "I don't want to talk too much about my own personal political beliefs," Micheal notes. "I think in politics, people have to put their egos to the side and work together." Even though he is undoubtedly a progressive, he claims to have a large number of conservative friends which he made while the Marines, who have given him an appreciation for and an understanding of conservative America. "When it comes to the Republican Party as a whole, I cannot agree with their platform and their values. But I can agree with things on an issue-by-issue basis, which is how people should work together."

On March 1, 2016, Micheal participated in history when he went to caucus for Bernie Sanders in the so-called "Super Tuesday." Known as one of the most influential nights of any United States presidential election cycle, 2016's "Super Tuesday" saw the states of Alabama, Arkansas, Colorado, Georgia, Massachusetts, Minnesota, Oklahoma, Tennessee, Texas, Vermont, and Virginia participate in the Democratic and Republican primaries through both elections and caucuses.

The night changed the course of the election. It was a big win for Donald Trump, who scored seven of the elections up for grabs; essentially putting the final nail in the coffin for Florida Senator Marco Rubio's presidential bid and dramatically slowing down Texas Senator Ted Cruz's momentum. For the Democrats, "Super Tuesday" was considered a big win for Hillary Clinton, who won seven of the 11 states and picked up 486 delegates. Colorado was one of the four states won by Bernie Sanders (along with Minnesota, Oklahoma, and Vermont), who carried the state by an over 8% margin.

Although Sanders pledged to keep fighting, and his supporters continued to be optimistic (perhaps, overly so), it became increasingly clear after "Super Tuesday" that Clinton was likely to win the Democratic nomination. This realization put many high-profile Sanders supporters in an uncomfortable position, especially in states like Colorado, which had clearly favored him over Clinton. According to Micheal, this is how he gained a foothold and recognition in the local political scene.

"It's all kind of a fluke, really," Micheal remembers. He didn't have much of a sense of the immense importance of the paperwork when he filled it out. "I completely did it on a whim. The Democrats had emailed me all these forms to become a state delegate, a national delegate, an elector—you name it. They were just these little PDFs and pretty easy to fill out. Really, the only qualification that you had to have was that you had to be over the age of 18." What Micheal did not realize when he sent the forms back was that he was one of the few Sanders supporters who had expressed willingness to vote for Clinton in the Electoral College.

Micheal would soon receive a life-changing call from a group of Colorado progressives. They were interested in meeting him to see if they would encourage their network to vote for him to become an elector. Within no time, they were sitting face-to-face at nearby Starbucks, and then conversing at length at a Korean barbecue restaurant. "I don't know what they saw in me," Micheal questions himself even now. "I guess I was a former veteran and working my way through school, so I looked like a solid choice." Indeed, he was securely in the Bernie camp, but seemed to be willing to toe the party line, if need be. By the end of the lunch, they told Micheal that they would support his candidacy for the Electoral College within their network, and prepared him for the fact that he might have a chance at winning.

"Everything happened so quickly," remembers Micheal. He designed some business cards that supported his candidacy to pass out to his fellow Democrats at the next gathering. "The idea of becoming an elector was really exciting to me because it meant that my signature would go into the Library of Congress. At the time, I was pretty certain that the Democrats would win the 2016 election, and I was inspired by the idea of becoming a part of history. You know, my mother isn't around anymore. The thought of having something live past me really motivated me."

On the day of the County Convention at a local high school, less than two weeks after "Super Tuesday," Micheal found himself winning the elector position, beating out local party bellwethers. "At the time, I had the full intention of voting for the Democratic nominee, even if it turned out to be Hillary Clinton. But I had also full faith in Bernie Sanders and that he was somehow going to be able to figure it out." From the County

Convention, Micheal went to the State Convention in Loveland in mid-April, where he was chosen as an alternate delegate to the Democratic National Convention that summer, which he also describes as something of a fluke. In fact, he had even left early to take his dog to the vet, thinking he did not have much of a chance. "I didn't really have any understanding of the whole process when I first started. I learned it as I went along."

As he headed to Philadelphia in late July, Micheal was filled with optimism, even though it was a financial sacrifice for him to even get there. He did not realize what a hornet's nest he was about to walk into, or how the results of the election would make him question the very nature of the Electoral College to which he had just been elected by his peers.

Bret Chiafalo
Part 1

"I am not a Democrat by choice. I am a Democrat by lack of choice," Bret Chiafalo, a 41-year-old native of Washington state asserts. "If there was a realistic party besides the Democratic Party on the left, I would join it in a second." In his mind a party isn't a legitimate party if it just rises up every four years for the presidential election; it needs local seats and state representatives to be sustainable. Although he readily admits that the more local politics is, the "crazier it is," Bret has a soft spot in his heart for politics at the grassroots level. He has participated in every Washington state Democratic caucus since he turned eighteen years old.

He came to his political beliefs by himself, growing up in a family that was just mildly political, perhaps leaning a bit to the right. "My parents fell to the libertarian side of things. Mostly they thought that the government didn't need to spend so much money," Bret says. His father was quite literally a rocket scientist working as part of the military industrial complex, with a stock portfolio that made sure that the family was in the upper-middle class. However, during the 1987 Black Monday stock market crash, the largest one-day drop of the Dow Jones index in history, his family found itself struggling a bit. His parents began to scale back and his mother, who had stayed home to raise him, started working as a real estate agent.

Despite the setback, the family was still securely in the middle class, with Bret beginning high school on Mercer Island, one of the 100 richest ZIP codes in the United States, nestled in between Redmond and Seattle. Although he was mostly exposed to the Republican way of thinking, he noticed social discrepancies that made him uncomfortable. He thought it was strange how all of the students drove their own fancy SUVs and Mercedes to school, while the teachers' parking lot was filled with beat-up economy cars. "I kept wondering to myself: how does a system like this make any sense at all?" Bret comments on the roots of his political awakening.

Bret admits that he had a difficult time fitting into the affluent high school. Not only was he a self-proclaimed "nerd" with ADHD, but also he had what he describes as an invisible disability called ulcerative colitis. Diagnosed at the ripe age of twelve with this disease that affects the large intestine, he suffered constant pain and cramping, which affected his peer relationships, as well as his school performance. When he discovered that he was qualified for a program called Running Start, which allowed him to take courses at the local community college while still in high school, he jumped at the chance to leave.

College classes transformed Bret and gave him a new sense of political understanding, as he was inspired by the texts of liberal scholar Noam Chomsky. Around the same time, Bret began smoking marijuana, which relieved the pain of his ulcerative colitis. He didn't understand why something so helpful could be illegal, so he researched the topic in-depth, an activity that he would come to do frequently as he grew older. "I was essentially a high school kid reading everything about medical marijuana I could find, and really technical things, too. I was trying to plow through and understand Harvard-published studies," Bret remembers. He got so engrossed in the topic that he lied about his age to make himself seem older, so that he could go and gather signatures for marijuana legalization.

Noting that he worked with a large number of libertarians for the legalization of marijuana, his political identity as a progressive was solidified in 1999 when he witnessed the protests against the World Trade Organization in Seattle. Now described as the "Battle of Seattle," over 40,000 people protested against the World Trade Organization's meeting in the city. Costing the city an estimated $20 million, these protests were one of the first major demonstrations against economic globalization and trade liberalization in the United States. "I was only eighteen years old at the time, but that completely galvanized me," Bret recalls. "I remember seeing everyone out there protesting peacefully. And then when these 500 or so anarchists did something, the cops and the media swooped in, making it all look like it was a riot. These were people trying to fight for their livelihoods and wanting to save the planet, and at the end of the day, their message didn't matter as much as some broken McDonald's windows."

Even though he ended up doing two years of college studies, Bret didn't finish his high school degree. (He later went back at the age of 25 to get his high school diploma and complete another year of community college.) Throughout his twenties, he found himself working a lot of crappy, minimum wage retail jobs. A release for him was political activism, as was his hobby of building gaming computers. One day, he decided to take an online gaming computer certification course and stumbled into the world of technology.

By the time he was in his thirties, things finally seemed like they were looking up for him; he had found his specialization in technology crisis management. He joined X-Box in their 24/7 operations center, where he watched the network and tried to put out fires when they arose. "You can think of it as a small-scale NASA mission control from the movies," he gushes. "Say, if an X-Box server went out in Japan, we would be there to get it back up-and-running. We would get the right engineers on the scene, organize translations, and manage communication messaging to our stakeholders, as well as the public."

When he started his job with X-Box, he purposefully distanced himself from politics so that he could put all of his focus on career advancement. Between 2013 and 2015, he wasn't active at all. However, once he heard Bernie Sanders announce his campaign for presidency, he was drawn back into the Democratic Party. When he began to volunteer in the campaign, he remembers feeling inspired. "I realized that so many people were out there fighting for the same thing, showing that not all Democrats are just corporatists," he says.

Bret proudly mentions that he was chosen as the Sanders captain for his precinct caucus. Describing himself as an extrovert, the caucus system was something that came naturally to Bret and something that he definitely looked forward to every four years. "I get a lot of personal fulfillment from the caucuses. It is great to be able to talk politics with all of the people in your ZIP code, even if you don't always agree," he raves. "Where else do you get to meet new neighbors and find out what is bothering them and what they are struggling with?"

Perhaps because of his own personal health struggles, Bret believes that America's biggest challenge is healthcare, noting that he was extremely disappointed when Obama's healthcare reform turned out to be what he describes as a version of Romneycare (named after the system developed by former Republican Massachusetts governor Mitt Romney), rather than a single-payer national healthcare system paid for by the government. "I don't think that anyone should have to choose between paying rent or paying for medication that a doctor prescribed," he comments. "Too many people are afraid of going to the doctor because they don't think that they can afford it." Bret believes himself to be one of the luckier ones in his generation—someone who has health insurance and just started his 401(k) retirement plan—despite not having a college degree.

Bret recognizes the limitations of Washington's caucus system—noting that he doesn't think that it will be able to survive much longer—by describing it as akin to an unattainable privilege for those less fortunate: "Its dark side is that it is not very accessible. If you are working two or three jobs just to make ends meet, what are the chances that you are going to be able to join all the levels of the caucus?"

It was at the Legislative District 21 Caucus that Bret first got the idea to become an elector. He was talking to a random person, who commented that they didn't know how electors in the Electoral College were chosen. Since he had been to so many caucuses, he recalled his past experiences. "The person just responded, 'Huh, that's interesting.' But for me, it really got me thinking," Bret says. "Everyone always made a big deal about running as a delegate for the Democratic National Convention. But nobody ever made a big deal about running as an elector." He was determined to find out why.

"Being a delegate is a really sexy job—you get to scream and fight for your candidate at the Convention and return home as the hero," he asserts. He knew that as a straight, middle class, cis white male, he had a tough shot at being chosen as a delegate—something that he accepts as a healthy development, noting that it is important that historically lesser-heard voices get attention. However, at the same time, he felt like he had something to offer the Democrats.

Leading up to the Congressional District Caucus, Bret started doing in-depth research about the Electoral College. He had always felt like he understood the Electoral College and was thoroughly opposed to it as an outmoded system that should be replaced by the popular vote. (Indeed, Bret recalls a college project about the Electoral College, in which he made a big stand for one-person, one-vote.) However, as Bret researched, he realized that there was a lot more to it. Describing himself as "an ideas guy who might have trouble sometimes following through on tasks," a new, slightly crazy idea began to formulate in his mind: he could run to be an elector.

As he was fundamentally against the Electoral College, there was no question of what his elector campaign platform was going to be: his personal disapproval of the Electoral College system. Having received a list of all the delegates who would be attending the Congressional District Caucus, he started calling them up during his spare time to ask for their support in his elector bid. As a Bernie supporter, he focused only on the Bernie delegates, who numbered somewhere between 70 and 90, hypothesizing that the Clinton delegates wouldn't be of much help.

"Most of the conversations began the same way: I had to explain what the elector position was. After that, I would ask them if they supported the Electoral College. Their answer was always 'no,'" Bret remembers. "I would tell them that I was running to be an elector on an anti-Electoral College platform and started listing my credentials." It was tough work to connect with all of them; some conversations only lasted a couple of minutes, while others would last half an hour or more.

On the day of the Congressional District Caucus in May, Bret thought he might actually have a shot to become the elector when he wrote his name down on the sign-up sheet. He had already done a lot of field work and he saw that there were only two other males and three females who had put their names in the hat. (The Democratic Party in Washington stipulates that the top male and the top female have a run-off.) Bret walked away feeling confident when he heard a caucus organizer yell out, "Anyone who wants to be an elector, come over here and sign up!" His heart dropped as he saw a long line forming in front of the table. At that moment, he believed that his chance of becoming an elector had just slipped through his fingers.

Indeed, instead of going up against just two other men, Bret had to go up against 30 to 40 men. The whole process lasted a couple of hours, as each individual was given the opportunity to make a one-and-a-half-minute speech. Bret forgot the details of his speech, noting that he did it in his signature, off-the-cuff style. However, he did feel like he got his anti-Electoral College message across.

What interested Bret was that most of the people whom he was running against had just run as delegates to the Democratic National Convention. Indeed, as the speeches for the electors were taking place, behind the scenes, volunteers were counting ballots to determine who were the winners of the delegate election. Tongue in cheek, Bret noticed that their speeches were uncannily similar, and he figured that they didn't quite understand what the difference was between a national delegate and an elector. "They were standing up there, saying things like, 'Vote for me because I support Bernie 100%,'" he laughs. "They didn't really understand what this elector position was all about."

Figuring that he didn't have a chance, Bret was shocked when he came out with the most votes in the male group. It was then that Bret discovered that he was about to meet his toughest challenger yet: the woman he faced in the run-off was none other than a Superdelegate, an unpledged delegate to the Democratic National Convention (a position normally given to party leaders and bellwethers, often thought to influence the results of the Convention itself.) The first two times the votes were counted, Bret and his opponent stood at a dead tie. For the third vote, Bret came out ahead, securing his position as an elector.

"I think that for a lot of caucuses, they just end up voting for whoever becomes the national delegate," Bret hypothesizes, still seemingly surprised that he was able to clinch the position. At the time, he had no plan for what would happen after he became an elector. But true to his nature, he dived into the topic with enthusiasm. "I am a giant nerd," he comments, "And I decided if I was an elector, I was going to jump into the Electoral College and give it my all."

The Twelfth Amendment

On September 19, 1796, a letter that would come to change the course of American politics was published in the *American Daily Advertiser*. Its author was none other than President George Washington (although large swaths of it were also penned by Founding Father Alexander Hamilton), who declined to pursue a third term as President.

It was doubtless a moment of uncertainty for the nascent nation, which had not yet experienced a transition of power. Washington had even considered stepping down after his first term, but was convinced to stay after hearing that the country needed his unifying presence for stability. While outside forces were certainly at play with respect to the nation's survival, equally destabilizing were the different political factions that were burgeoning, particularly when it came to the Federalist and

Democratic-Republican parties. In his letter, Washington warned against the rise of factionalism, saying:

> *However [political parties] may now and then answer popular ends,*
> *they are likely in the course of time and things, to become potent engines,*
> *by which cunning, ambitious, and unprincipled men will be enabled to*
> *subvert the power of the people and to usurp for themselves the reins of*
> *government, destroying afterwards the very engines which have lifted*
> *them to unjust dominion.*

The 1796 election would also prove to be the first test of the mechanism that the Founders developed in the 1787 Constitutional Convention in Philadelphia to find a new leader for the executive branch—a mechanism that they called the Electoral College. For months, the early thought and opinion leaders of the United States had debated how to determine the new President. At the time, no other country in the world had a mechanism to elect their executive leader, so there were no examples to follow, and the conversations were fraught with anxiety.

The delegates at the Constitutional Convention were concerned with having a balance of power between the three branches of government, so the idea that Congress could pick a leader was ultimately rejected. Suggestions to enact a popular vote were also rejected, in part due to the fear that it would create a "democratic mob." Other concerns about the popular vote also stemmed from the practical issues of developing an electoral system in the 18th century, such as lack of communication and transportation mechanisms. The delegates were concerned that state populations would vote in their "hometown favorite," regardless of whether or not he was a good pick for the presidency, simply because they did not have adequate information about other choices.

The compromise was for each state to decide on its own independent electors to cast ballots for the presidency. The number of electors that each state had was the combined numbers of how many senators and House of Representatives members each state had, giving states with smaller populations more weight in the process. Each state was given the autonomy to choose electors at its own discretion. Indeed, in the early days, many electors were decided by the state legislatures. Choosing electors by popular vote only began to gain traction in the early 19th century.

The hope was that the individuals chosen to be electors would be esteemed members of their communities and well versed about national politics. In spite of this, the Founding Fathers put restrictions on the electors—they were each provided with two votes for the President, with the caveat that at least one of their choices for President must be a candidate who belonged to another state.

For the first two elections under the Electoral College, there was no real competition for the presidency—George Washington won each time without much contention. The real debate was on who would be the Vice President, and John Adams was Washington's Vice President. However, the 1796 election without George Washington's candidacy was different, and had the opportunity to expose potential flaws in the system.

Before the creation of political parties, the Founders did not believe that one individual candidate would be able to get a clear majority of Electoral College votes—the only exception being a clear unifying figure like George Washington. In the case that a majority was not achieved, they had created a distinct and at times complicated plan that would allow the matter to be solved in the House of Representatives—a scenario called a "contingent election." Essentially, if no one candidate won a majority, the top five people who had garnered the most Electoral College votes would be recommended to the House of Representatives, where each state would have one single vote. The person with the most votes would then become President, while the person with the second-largest number of votes would become Vice President.

The creation of political parties would transform how the system operated, and the 1796 election proved how disastrous the Electoral College in its original form could be. The presidential election saw the newly-formed Federalist Party (which put forth John Adams as its candidate) and the Democratic-Republican Party (which put forth Thomas Jefferson as its candidate) at each other's throats, with insults thrown left and right. Additionally, the mobilization of parties across state lines ensured that a candidate could actually receive a majority of votes, despite Washington's absence.

Vice President John Adams was elected President in 1796 with 71 electoral votes. By carrying the majority of the Northeastern states, Adams had gotten one extra vote to give him a majority in the Electoral College. Unfortunately, his arch-rival Thomas Jefferson received 68 votes in the Electoral College, giving him the place of the Vice President. With a President belonging to the Federalist Party and a Vice President belonging to the Democratic-Republican Party, it soon became clear that the Electoral College system was ultimately flawed, as the two leaders used their positions to undermine each other, especially in terms of foreign policy.

The flaws of the early Electoral College system became brazenly evident again in the 1800 election, which saw President Adams and Vice President Jefferson once again competing for power. Sometimes referred to as the "Revolution of 1800," that year's presidential race had extraordinary implications for both national and global politics. American legal scholar and University of Texas Law School professor Sanford Levinson describes it as one of the most significant events in world history, as "it represented the first time that an incumbent leader was defeated in an election." Although there was no doubt that Adams lost the election (becoming the first one-term President in United States history, and also setting the precedent for a defeated leader to step down), the election had additional implications for the evolution of the early Electoral College system.

To avoid the challenges that inevitably arose with a President and a Vice President from different parties, both the Federalists and the Democratic-Republicans decided to promote a "party ticket" rather than individual candidates. John Adams's running mate was South Carolinian Charles C. Pinckney, while Thomas Jefferson's vice presidential pick was New Yorker Aaron Burr. The Federalists were well organized, ensuring that Adams would receive one more vote than Pinckney, so that Adams received 65 votes to Pinckney's 64. Unfortunately, the Democratic-Republicans were not nearly so organized. Perhaps it was the poor methods of communication of the era, or perhaps the strategy and rules of the Electoral College were completely overlooked, but Thomas Jefferson and his running mate Aaron Burr ended up with the exact same number of votes—73 each.

This was extremely problematic, as it meant that the President and the Vice-President had to be determined in the House of Representatives. Many Federalist representatives held quite acrimonious feelings towards Jefferson, as they believed that he thwarted their efforts during his tenure as Vice-President over the previous four years. As each of the sixteen states in the union were given one vote, an absolute majority of nine states was required. Six of the eight Federalist states decided to back Burr's presidency as a form of protest against Thomas Jefferson, while Jefferson had the backing of eight states. Two states, Maryland and Vermont, cast blank ballots after being unable to come up with a consensus.

From February 11 to 17 of 1801, it was unclear who would be the President and who would be the Vice President. Burr was certainly under pressure to step down, but he did not seem to be opposed to the idea of becoming the President himself, which he carefully insinuated in private letters. Each day, the vote was recounted, and each day, the vote remained the same. There was no clear winner. In the meantime, the uncertainty was certainly having some lingering effects in the efficacy of the political system. Supposedly, the governors of Pennsylvania and Virginia (both of which supported Jefferson, and the latter of which was his home state) were so fed up that they were "threatening to call out their state militias and order them to march on the new national capital."

It is pure speculation what domestic conflicts would have arisen if the status quo had remained. The early United States had Alexander Hamilton to thank for bringing an end to the tenuous situation. Of course, his involvement was not so much a vote of confidence for Jefferson, but rather based on his continued animosity toward Aaron Burr (which ultimately led to a duel some four years later, when the then-Vice President Burr shot Hamilton, who died from the injuries the following day.) Although a staunch Federalist, Hamilton decided to jump into the debate and started a rigorous letter-writing campaign that ultimately shifted the balance of politics to Jefferson's favor.

Realizing that the current system was unsustainable, the Democratic-Republican government, under Jefferson, made electoral reform a top priority. They waited until after a new Congress was voted in during the last two years of Jefferson's first term, so that they had a majority in both the Senate and the House of Representatives.

One of the reasons that Jefferson was careful to wait was because he knew that changing the Electoral College system would take some political capital, as it required amending the Constitution of the United States. Although both parties could agree that the system was problematic, they disagreed on how they might change it, afraid that a change could give one side an edge over the other.

The Electoral College before the 12ᵗʰ Amendment

A TALE OF 2 ELECTIONS

1796

PRESIDENT
John Adams
Federalist

71 votes

THE PROBLEM:
The candidate with the most Electoral College votes became President, while the one with the second most votes became Vice President.

What would happen if the President and the Vice President belonged to two different parties?

VICE-PRESIDENT
Thomas Jefferson
Democratic-Republican

68 votes

THE IMPACT:
The Adams/Jefferson administration was marked by political conflict. Adams became the nation's first one-term President.

1800
IT'S A TIE!

PRESIDENTIAL CANDIDATE
Thomas Jefferson
Democratic-Republican

73 votes

THE PROBLEM:
In the case of a tie, there was a contingent election in the House of Representatives.

What would happen if the losing Federalist party tried to deny Jefferson his presidential win?

VICE-PRESIDENTIAL CANDIDATE
Aaron Burr
Democratic-Republican

73 votes

THE IMPACT:
After political chaos, Jefferson won the contingent election. The Electoral College was reformed by the 12th Amendment to incorporate the development of party tickets.

The first change that the Amendment noted was that votes for President and Vice-President would be two separate contests—an implicit recognition of the evolution and development of political parties within the American political system. Although all members of Congress had since taken one side or another, at least a few recognized that this could ultimately be problematic. Federalist Senator Samuel White of Delaware thought that this would ultimately lead to electors not considering vice presidential candidates because of their capacities and virtues, but rather for their ability to play the political game, saying that eventually the question would be: "Can he by his name, by his connection, by his wealth, by his local situation, by his influence, or [by] his intrigues best promote the election of a President?"

Another major point of contention might seem relatively unimportant by today's standards, but was still important to the Founders who originally devised the Electoral College system. In the case of no candidate receiving the majority of the Electoral College votes, three (instead of the original five) top candidates would be brought to the House of Representatives to determine who would become the President.

Small-population Federalist states were nervous that this made it less likely that a candidate from a small state might be referred to the House of Representatives and considered for the office. Indeed, the divisions among large and small states seemed to take center-stage, with the Federalists preparing a defense that included revisiting the ethically problematic three-fifths clause in the Constitution (which counted each African American slave as three-fifths of a person), thereby affecting the balance of power of slaveholding states in both the House of Representatives and the Electoral College. In spite of a rigorous debate about Electoral College reform, which lasted 11 hours on December 2, 1803, the Federalists ultimately failed. It passed through the Senate 22–10 and was approved by the House of Representatives 84–42 on December 9, 1803.

For the proposed amendment to become a reality, it had to then be approved by the state legislatures of two-thirds of the states. Over the next six months, one state after another ratified it. On June 15, 1804, it was ratified by New Hampshire, making it the Twelfth Amendment to the U.S. Constitution. Unsurprisingly, the small-population states of the Northeast were unwilling to jump on board. It was rejected by both Delaware and Connecticut, and the Massachusetts legislature only ratified it in 1961.

With the ratification of the Twelfth Amendment, it looked like political parties were entrenched within the political system, dispelling any administrations plagued by political differences, like the Adams-Jefferson administration. It also ensured that embarrassing (and potentially disarming) situations, like a tie for President between Burr and Jefferson, were out of the question. While the Electoral College had successfully adapted to a new era, it was clear that the amendment was going to change the course of the Electoral College forever, and not necessarily in a way that the Founders intended it to be.

Art Sisneros
Part 1

Art Sisneros's life transformed when he became a Christian at the age of twenty-eight. At the time, he was working in Houston's restaurant industry, an environment which he describes as toxic. After getting off work late, he would go out with his colleagues and party until the next morning. He was drinking heavily and started getting into drugs.

He had gone straight into the restaurant industry after high school. Although he had been accepted into a couple of colleges, he didn't know what sort of career he wanted to pursue, so he let the opportunities for higher education pass him by. Art now describes his former life as a "downhill spiral" that was "without hope." With no energy to change his behavior or his job, he woke up day after day and repeated what had happened the day before.

When he shared his feelings with a coworker, she mentioned that she had gone to church the Sunday before and that it might help him deal with his depressed feelings. Art's parents were not Christians and he had not grown up going to church (even for Christmas or Easter services), so it was a new idea for him. While his colleague would only end up going to church a few more Sundays before returning to business as usual, the church she suggested would prove to be the lifeline that Art so desperately wanted.

As he was walking out of church that first Sunday, the pastor touched his shoulder and asked him what he was doing the next day. Art replied that he didn't have anything planned and found himself sitting around the dinner table with the pastor and his family the following evening. "The whole next six months were spent with the pastor, being exposed to God's word," Art comments. "I was discovering something that I had never seen before—something bigger than myself. And it changed my life."

His life transformation was solidified when, nine months after becoming a Christian, he met his wife through a missionary organization based in Texas. He had volunteered to host a Muslim teacher from Indonesia, who was receiving training in Houston during the summer. When the organization held a dinner with all of the hosting volunteers and hosted teachers, Art found himself sitting at the same table as a beautiful accountant, who was hosting a few Muslim teachers from Uzbekistan in her home. As she was originally from Indonesia, the conversation flowed between herself, Art, and his guest from Indonesia. Once the teachers returned to their home countries, they stayed in contact. The rest, they might say, is history (although Art notes that they had an unusually long engagement of a year and a half, as they brought her parents over from Indonesia for the wedding.)

With his new faith and a new wife to support him, Art transitioned from the pervasive party atmosphere in the restaurant industry into the oil and gas industry, in which he worked as an industrial welding machinery salesman. When they started thinking about a family, Art and his wife decided to let their Christian convictions drive their journey into parenthood. Art's wife volunteered to give up her job to become a full-time homeschooling mom. With only one income, they downsized to a smaller, more affordable area outside of Houston called Dayton. A small city of only 7,500 people located in Liberty County, Dayton's claim to fame was a 1980 UFO sighting, after which a local who claimed that she had sustained injuries sued the United States Air Force, apparently for a cover-up. Art and his wife found that life in Dayton suited them well, eventually joining a small, conservative Presbyterian Church, where much of the congregation also homeschools its children.

Now 43 years old, Art has six children, the oldest of whom is thirteen, and the youngest, nine months. He and his wife intend to homeschool them all. Although his wife does much of the teaching herself, he likes to jump in to teach a class or two each week, normally focusing on history or government. As I talk with Art, he somehow seems to steer most conversations back to his children, and describes how he turns everything into a teaching moment, whether it is being late for dinner because of a networking event ("teaching how to apologize") or trying for a promotion ("showing how to work hard and accomplish a goal.") It seems like everything in the Sisneros household is an educational opportunity.

Art comments that lately a lot of their life revolves around food, with one of their children determined to study in France to become a world-class chef. "If that is what he wants, I want to give him the tools to make that happen. We are complete foodies," he says. "Right now, we are making our own sausages, smoking our own meats, and baking our own breads. It is a lot less stressful than politics."

Art came about his interest in politics later in life. He grew up in a non-religious, completely apolitical household. Although his Hispanic parents had grown up speaking Spanish themselves, they were purposeful in not introducing Hispanic social issues or even the Spanish language to their son. "I think it was a product of the age," Art comments, noting that his parents thought it would be helpful if he couldn't speak Spanish. "When I was growing up, it was maybe a bit of a negative thing to speak Spanish in Texas. Everyone looked at you like you were a Mexican or an American; you couldn't be both."

Art doesn't remember his mother ever going out to vote when he was a child. He is not sure if that is because she didn't have political opinions of her own, or if she just didn't talk about them very much. His parents divorced when he was ten years old. Afterwards, his mother started working and was not home much. His father worked in a nearby chemical plant. "My dad always voted for the Democrats. But I don't think he did it because he was really political. He was more of like, 'I am in the union. And us union people, we need to stick together and vote Democrat,'" Art recalls. He says that if there was any political message in his childhood home, it was: Democrats are for the working people and Republicans are for the rich people.

Art was likewise apolitical in his early adult life. When I asked him about the 2000 election and how that might have affected his later opinions on the Electoral College, he comments, "I did read about it—I was always a huge reader. But it didn't mean that much to me back then." After becoming a Christian, Art began to believe that he needed to adopt a whole new worldview that accompanied his new faith; he needed to find a new paradigm by which to live his life. "I was reading and devouring everything that I could get my hands on when I came across some materials about the Austrian School of economics," he remembers of his first introduction to the free market economic school of thought.

"It just made sense to me. I realized that I could have a coherent world-view that was consistent with my Christian faith. Politics and economics didn't have to conflict with Christianity." Incorporating historical economic thinkers like Ludwig von Mises and Friedrich Hayek, Austrian economics stipulates that the less government intervention there is in the economic market, the better the outcome. (Austrian economics has seen a bit of a resurgence in the last couple of decades after the founding of the Mises Institute think tank in 1982, which uses Austrian economics as a means of supporting libertarian-leaning policies.)

Art believed that emphasizing the power of the individual rather than the government when it came to economics was deeply empowering. "As a Christian, I could have compassion for the poor and for people of other nations. I could say that the United States conducting endless wars was hurting populations around the globe," he remarks. "But I realized that compassion was best coming from individuals, families, church communities, and private corporations—not from the state." Austrian economics provided a much-neeeded perspective, as he had been attempting to come to terms with his feelings after traveling to rural Indonesia to visit the Muslim teacher he had previously hosted in his home. The experience had dramatically expanded his understanding of the world.

"The capital of Jakarta was as nice as New York City," he comments, "But then we got to this little remote village, where people were still growing rice without any modern equipment." Alongside the Indonesian teacher, he visited small Islamic schools in the countryside, acting as a guest speaker of sorts and helping the children with their English. The memory feels fresh in Art's mind—and not just because he took all of his kids to Indonesia two years ago—but because it was a teaching moment for himself. "The people there had a sense of contentment. They knew what they didn't have, but they didn't let it affect their outlook on life."

Likewise, when I ask Art how he would compare himself to his peers, it is clear that he shares a similar type of contentment, although he kind of shrugs the question off. He notes that he and his wife are able to make things work on one income, so they are clearly in the middle-class spectrum. "I chose such a different lifestyle for myself and for my family. I don't really think that there is anyone else in my peer group who is home-schooling six kids," he says. "I can't really compare myself with others."

With his newfound knowledge of Austrian economics and free markets, when Art discovered Ron Paul's 2008 campaign for President, he was captivated. "Here you have this humble, non-authoritative type of person running for President," he remembers. "He wasn't charismatic at all, but his message resonated." Art quickly jumped on board with his fellow Texan's campaign. However, after Paul's failed presidential bid, he didn't stick around in the local political scene.

When Paul ran again in 2012, Art was keen to jump in to help his campaign, as well as to stay engaged in local politics afterward. Art claims that a big part of why he wanted to remain engaged in politics was because he and his wife were just starting to homeschool their oldest son, and he was thinking about how he was going to teach his children government and politics. "I was just starting to understand the limitations of the home-school curriculum. You have some curriculum that is good and you have some that is bad. You really have to dig around," he comments. "I was wondering, how was I going to teach politics to my children? Because I knew that when it comes to politics, how it actually works is a lot different from how it should work."

Once Art started attending local meetings, he was surprised that he could make a big impact. He was a bit irked at the Texas Republican Party, which he describes as "a private club with its own private rules," and was equally irked by the Republican establishment's dismissal of Ron

Paul, commenting that he was shocked when a group at CPAC booed Paul after he described Jesus Christ as a "peacekeeper" in the same context that the United States should not be involved in wars overseas. As Art started showing up to local political meetings, he discovered that he wasn't the only one who felt that way. In fact, Ron Paul had brought a lot of like-minded people into the Republican Party. Art recalls that it was pretty easy for them to find each other: "Basically, you showed up to one of these local meetings, and if you saw somebody else in the room who was under the age of 65, you probably had a lot in common. You probably both supported Ron Paul."

Art found himself a part of a small, close-knit group that would support each other in local political initiatives. "If we could all get to the same meeting, we could have a lot of influence," Art comments. "We could actually end up changing races. But for us, it was more important to get the liberty message out. We always focused on whether the candidate supported strengthening the state or advancing the liberty of individuals and their families." Together, they would show up at anything from elections for school boards and sheriffs to commissioners' court. Art recalls that in those early days, they were just trying to make some noise. They started a podcast called The Liberty Line and even began to start organizing a pro-life platform called Abolition Abortion.

Through all of his activism, Art felt like he was going up against the establishment a lot. He and his friends found themselves threatened by party bellwethers, but paid them no heed. He felt supported by the grassroots nature of the Texas Republican Party, which always allowed him opportunities to participate, even if he didn't always agree with the leadership. "Everything in the platform is decided and voted on at the state convention. I actually agree with most of our platform. I just think that a lot of Texas Republican politicians don't follow it," he comments.

By the time 2016 came around, Art was excited to join his third state convention. He had come from a non-political background and was now one of the delegates chosen to go to the convention to determine the platform for the next year. For someone who had dived headfirst into politics after Paul's 2012 bid, it was incredibly exciting to pursue this new interest. Commenting that most people didn't have the time to be involved in party politics, he knew that he was just going to be around "nerds like [himself] and politicos and political wonks for days on end," but he was looking forward to making his voice heard within the Republican Party.

David Mulinix
Part 1

David Mulinix wakes up early on Sunday, just as he has almost every Sunday for the last eight years, to start cooking a massive feast alongside his wife, Sherry. That evening, they deliver the food to a group of nearly 100 homeless people gathered in Thomas Square in Honolulu, as a part of a coordinated effort of four families to try to make a dent in Hawaii's pressing homelessness problem. Deemed a "crisis" by media outlets, Hawaii has one of the highest per capita homelessness rates in the United States.

Activism is clearly a bond that holds David and Sherry together. When I ask David what he likes to do in his spare time, he struggles to list hobbies, but instead rambles off a list of initiatives which he started alongside his wife, a nutrition specialist. It comes as no surprise when David later shares how they first met: working together at the Alliance for Survival, an anti-nuclear group out of California. David was one of the "small hand-ful of organizers," while Sherry was a university volunteer.

"It was back when we used to have something called 'phone trees' to mobilize people rapidly," explains the 70-year-old non-profit manage-ment professional. "Basically, I would call ten people, and those ten people would call ten other people with the information about where and when to protest. And those ten people would reach out to ten more. It was the quickest way to get the message out to 1,000 people." David was organizing a protest against nuclear weapons being stored across the street from an elementary school in Seal Beach, California, when he bumped into Sherry, who was there to protest after getting his message through the phone tree. It could be said that the rest is history.

Until about a year ago, when Whole Foods offered to sponsor the project by giving food that they would have otherwise thrown away, David, Sherry, and the other volunteers used to foot the bill for all of the grocer-ies to feed the homeless themselves. "It is kind of fun," David comments. "Before we show up to Whole Foods that morning, we have no idea what sort of groceries we are going to get. Then, we have to think on our toes about the best way to prepare it, divide up the work, and go back to our four separate kitchens and get cooking." By 5 P.M., dinner is served and David can relax. He normally brings his guitar and starts strumming and singing, infusing the meal with a sense of festivity. He describes it glow-ingly as a "picnic in the park."

David's passion project of feeding the homeless is a remnant of his stint as one of the founders of DeOccupy Honolulu, a part of Hawaii's Occupy Movement. He noticed that many homeless people joined the protestors with their own tents, claiming that the Occupy camp was the safest place for them in the city, as there weren't any drugs or alcohol around. As protestors and homeless people shared stories, activists became increasingly aware of Hawaii's homelessness problem, which included police abuse. "Police would raid communities of homeless people at something like 3 A.M. to 5 A.M.," David shares. "They would take everything from tents to clothes. They would also take things that are really problematic to replace, like children's school IDs and class textbooks and throw them into big dumpsters."

David is proud that he has played a role in not one but two lawsuits that have since been brought forth against the mayor for his so-called "compassionate disruption" approach towards Hawaii's homeless (which has been criticized as "criminalizing" homelessness by the website ThinkProgress.) "The police and the local government were trying to hide the issue of homelessness from all of the tourists who come to Hawaii. I mean, people come because they want to enjoy a slice of paradise—and homelessness doesn't fit with that narrative," David impassionedly notes. "Before the Occupy Movement, a lot of people didn't realize how abusive the system was toward the homeless."

David helped maintain the DeOccupy Honolulu encampment for two years. The camp in Thomas Square ended up becoming the longest continuously running Occupy encampment in the United States (he blames the movement's demise on President Obama's "screwing over the movement by coordinating the destruction of the camps.") As DeOccupy Honolulu took on local initiatives and goals—rather than just solely focusing on the big banks and Wall Street—David believes that the movement really gained legs in the state.

The name "DeOccupy" was in and of itself a local invention. Suggested by his encampment co-founder, a Kanaka Maoli Native Hawaiian activist, it alluded to the desire for national sovereignty felt by many Native Hawaiians, who believe that the United States had ulterior motives to occupy their land when the government provided assistance in the overthrow of the Hawaiian Kingdom in 1893. Indeed, this independence movement exploded soon after during 2014's Thirty Meter Telescope protests, when the locally-revered Mauna Kea mountain was chosen as the location for a new telescope.

Although it is precisely his distrust of the police that makes David such a powerful advocate and activist for the homeless, this feeling stems from a deeply painful chapter of his childhood in rural Ohio. When he was nine years old, his widowed mother remarried a man who beat her frequently—to the point that the police were called many times to the home. "This was when wives were still considered the property of their husbands. A man could violently force himself on his wife without consequences," David remembers.

Each time the police arrived, the incident was categorized as a domestic dispute that the man of the house needed to work out with his woman, leaving young David both flabbergasted and frustrated by their inaction. "The police only came to stop the disruption, not to protect my mother. It was then that I learned that I could never count on the police for protection. The police are there to protect buildings and streets. They are there to protect the government and the things that people own. Their priority is not ordinary people."

Although David shares such intimate stories of hardship, he still talks about the bulk of his childhood in Alliance, Ohio, in positive terms. His grandfather had traveled there from Freesoil, Michigan, determined to land a job in the city's growing manufacturing industry and leave behind the legacy of a seventh-generation family farm. Even though most of the men in his family worked at the local steel mill, David recounts the picturesque landscapes of his childhood, describing the cornfields surrounding his neighborhood and a dairy farm just down the road. "I lived in a town that looked like it came out of a Norman Rockwell painting—old red brick buildings, large family gatherings around the dinner table, and kids running barefoot through pastures with their trusty dogs."

In spite of this idyllic imagery, David believes that his childhood was problematic from a political perspective. "There was only one black kid at my school," he remembers, "and I recently learned that one of my great-aunts was actually a member of the Ku Klux Klan. I just had no clue." Although David unequivocally falls on the progressive scale of politics, it is this background to which he constantly returns when discussing the American conservative movement. "If everything and everyone around you support your opinions and ideas, it is hard for you to question yourself," he comments, "And most people believe things because they were raised to believe them; you cannot change their minds."

Besides his rocky family life, young David was also prone to illness: when he was thirteen years old, he had life-saving open-heart surgery. It was only due to new medical technology that he was able to escape the fate of this father, who had died of a heart attack just six years prior. Heart disease certainly shaped the course of David's life: although it ensured that he wouldn't be drafted for the Vietnam War, it also set him on a decades-long journey to explore his family legacy, without the guidance of his father. While his mother was of Irish and German descent, his father was a mix of Scandinavian, French, British, as well as the Cherokee, Lenape, and the Potawatomi Native American tribes.

"Because my father died when I was so young, I didn't have a male example to follow," David notes. "And I was not in a community with any indigenous elders to teach me my heritage." As a young boy, he tried to counter this by reading all the books that he could get about Native Americans from the library, finding inspiration in books about leaders like 19th-century chief Tecumseh. Recognizing his growing expertise, the librarian asked him to write reviews of new book acquisitions about

Native Americans. David was thrilled by the task and was proud when the librarian pasted his reviews inside the front covers.

David was also influenced by key Native Americans he met throughout his childhood, particularly the Cherokee heart surgeon who not only saved his life, but also provided him with a much-needed connection to the Cherokee culture. In spite of the daily hardships, David found that "connecting with my heritage helped me get over my father's death. It wasn't like I lost my father after all; my father was in the trees and the sky and I could talk to him whenever I wanted."

As he got closer to his Native American heritage, his anti-establishment streak was certainly solidified. He learned the stories of his Potawatomi ancestors, who had settled "living as white men" in Indiana when they were removed by the local militia in 1838 and relocated to Kansas, in an event called the Potawatomi Trail of Death. "When I read that, I had this feeling that the United States government couldn't be trusted. Treaties are made by the government, but they also can be broken by the government."

He views himself as a modern-day indigenous warrior, making a stand to take care of the people. "Socialism is like a tribe; helping each other in a big family. Capitalism is the exact opposite; there are a few people at the top and they don't help anybody," David outlines his political beliefs. Although vocalizing these ideas is relatively easy, David seems to be attempting something much more difficult: actually living by these principles. The list of causes he has dedicated himself to in the past is lengthy: protesting the Vietnam War; being an EMS worker and an anti-nuclear activist; running blood banks for the Red Cross; serving as the first executive director of Hawaii's Habitat for Humanity; organizing fundraisers for drama and science education programs in Hawaii's smaller islands, as well as for a new emergency room; organizing an Occupy Movement; and being one of the founders of Our Revolution Hawaii, an organization ideated by Bernie Sanders to help support progressive political movements. He and his wife also founded 350 Hawaii, a movement to help tackle climate change.

Before the 2016 presidential election, David was engaged in grassroots social projects, but largely distanced himself from party politics because he believed that there was no political party that represented his beliefs. "In my mind, the Democratic Party became the Republican Party when Bill Clinton was in power. The Democrats used to be funded by labor unions, but Clinton introduced neoliberalism as a tenet of the Party, and supported NAFTA. Naturally with NAFTA, all of the union jobs then got sent overseas," David explains. "Everything became rigged for the rich."

Little did David know, but one of his former colleagues at the antinuclear organization Alliance for Survival, a man named Tim Carpenter, was thinking the same thing. Carpenter founded Progressive Democrats for America, with the belief that he could transform the Democratic Party by bringing it back to its working-class roots. Right before his death from melanoma in 2014 at the age of 55, Carpenter had gotten 11,000 signatures of support for what was then considered a radical and far-fetched idea: the Vermont Independent Senator Bernie Sanders running as a Democrat presidential candidate. Several progressive news outlets reported that Sanders was so moved by Carpenter's tenacity in getting the signatures even in the face of death that he began to seriously explore a potential presidential bid.

David knew none of this background story when he heard Bernie Sanders on a progressive radio show; he would learn about Jim's involvement only later. But after only a few minutes of listening to Bernie talk, David decided to jump in wholeheartedly. "I am a total independent," David claims, "but I registered as a Democrat just so that I could help Bernie win." By the time 2015 had rolled around, David was on the ground for Bernie. "I would go and do my 9-to-5 day job. After work, I would just make phone calls and organize on social media. This has always been who I am and what I do."

However, it soon became clear that the new progressive converts to Hawaii's Democratic Party were not going to be met with open arms. "The side that supports the Clintons had an old boys club and they really weren't open to young progressives," David notes. Following Bernie's call to create a movement by increasing the number of progressives in leadership roles in the Democratic Party, the influx of new recruits "decided run for everything—every county committee, every state committee. That was the only way that our movement could be sustainable. And that is how my name got in the hat to become an elector."

At the state convention, David was manning the Sanders for President information table when a friend congratulated him for being elected as an elector. "I remember asking him, 'You mean I was chosen as an actual elector in the Electoral College?'" David comments. "I was so surprised. I didn't even remember that I had run for it. Although I was confused, I realized that my friends had given me a great honor. Other people had lobbied hard—and here I did nothing. I didn't even know that I had signed up to run. And I won."

As David began to think about how he had gotten chosen as an elector, he reasoned that "I had worked so hard for progressive causes in Hawaii for so long that I guess people knew me and trusted me." At first, the thought of being elected made him feel good, but then he realized that he was in a bit of a quandary: he was now an elector, but he didn't believe in the Electoral College. It was something that he would be much more comfortable protesting against than being part of.

Bill Greene
Part 2

Bill Greene thought that he might have a 50/50 shot of getting to be a Texas elector—and that would be the best-case scenario. Having just moved from Georgia a few years prior, he knew he was at a distinct disadvantage. However, at the same time, he thought that Texas might just be his saving grace.

Bill was hopeful because he believed that the Texas culture focusing on independence could influence even something as rigid as party hierarchy. In other states, the party leadership or an executive committee often just handpicks members to be electors. Not only is it considered a useful tool to honor the party faithful, but also, it ensures that the electors are more likely to be amenable to party leadership. In Bill's mind, this system was incredibly skewed toward former elected officials and big donors. By contrast, the fact that Texas even had a mechanism for

Bill to put his hat in the ring as an elector was extremely exciting to him. Even now, as he describes his bid at the Texas Republican State Convention, he says that he feels "humbled" by the knowledge that an ordinary person such as himself had a way of becoming an elector.

Indeed, the Founding Fathers viewed electors as extremely important for choosing the President. In his Federalist No. 68, Founding Father Alexander Hamilton (who wrote under the pseudonym Publius) described electors as "men most capable of analyzing the qualities adapted to the station, and acting under circumstances favorable to deliberation, and to a judicious combination of all the reason and inducements which were proper to govern their choice." Of course, Hamilton was writing these words in 1788—before the creation of political parties, a development in American politics that would place party loyalty over personal discernment as a qualification for an elector.

"Texas has a special grassroots culture, even when it comes to party politics," Bill asserts. "Quite literally, every single platform issue is voted upon. Delegates to the State Convention pick their own electors at the convention, according to their congressional districts." Bill knows that he would not even have had a chance of getting chosen to be a part of the delegation to attend the Republican National Convention in Cleveland, Ohio that July, as he wasn't connected enough in Texas. He was happy that he had already checked that off his bucket list years before. Although the position as a delegate comes with considerably more financial responsibilities, it also comes with the glitz and glamour of politics, celebrity, and power. Most people view it as, if not a greater honor, at least much more fun than being an elector.

When talking with Bill, I appreciate the precision and detail that he puts into describing exactly what his bid for an elector was like. While others sometimes seem to be hazy on the details, Bill clearly had a plan and set himself up as best he could for success in an election. Indeed, while I was researching this book, I became increasingly interested by one thing—that almost all of the electors who had gone rogue and with whom I had spoken ran their own campaigns to be elected by their peers, rather than chosen by their parties.

Bill claims that his electoral bid was helped by the fact that the Texas Republican leadership was unprepared. "The leadership within my congressional district had handpicked the chair of one of the county parties to be an elector," he remarks. "Normally, there weren't any contests for an elector, so, they were really surprised." Texas has 38 Electoral College votes; 36 of the electors are chosen according to votes by delegates from their respective congressional district, while the final two (which can be viewed as representing the state's two senators) are voted on at large during the course of the Republican Convention.

Living in Hidalgo County alongside the Mexican border, widely regarded as one of the fastest growing counties in the United States, Bill was not coming from a well-developed Republican stronghold when seeking the electorship. Bill carefully explains the details of how many delegates a county can send to the Republican State Convention—which is based on how many Republicans voted for governor in the last election, a special formula that only applies to the state of Texas. For Bill, this meant that he only had to convince a smaller caucus of some 60–70 individuals to back him, as he came from a congressional district which typically leans heavily toward the Democratic Party. At other caucuses with more Republican organization and leadership, he would have had a much more difficult time having to convince hundreds of delegates of his merits as a potential elector.

Another factor that may have played a role was that, at least according to Bill, the Republican State Convention was in a state of disarray.

He admits that a big part of that sentiment was what was happening nationwide: Democrats were divided between a party bellwether and a rogue independent candidate, while Republicans had been divided between seventeen distinct candidates, among whom businessman Donald Trump had managed to take the lead.

In Texas, Donald Trump's seemingly impossible rise had other implications: based on the conversations that Bill was having with some of his fellow Texas Republicans, he realized that Texas Senator Ted Cruz had a fighting chance. Cruz was certainly still the hometown favorite, after having won the March 1 Texas Republican primary by a bit less than 500,000 votes. During the State Convention, Bill certainly had the feeling that there were many more Cruz supporters on the ground than there were Trump supporters.

Later in our conversations, Bill commented on how strange it was to see all of the Cruz supporters very quickly switch over to the Trump side, especially when considering the nationwide movements (from the fly-by-the-seat-of-your-pants Change.Org and MoveOn online petitions to a slightly more coordinated Hamilton Electors movement) that was about to ensue to convince them switch their votes.

"When an elector votes, that person needs to vote their conscience," he comments. "I am not saying that other Republicans didn't vote their conscience. I am saying that when they decided to vote their conscience, for whatever reason, their conscience led them to vote for their party's chosen one." By then, many of the previously diehard Cruz supporters had become diehard Trump supporters, wearing MAGA hats. Bill speculates, that "it is interesting because they really did not start out that way. I think that it was the pushback from the Democrats and the Hillary supporters that forced the Republican Party to close its ranks. The Democrats overplayed their hand and it backfired."

Bill decided to make his run for elector as professional as he could. He wrote up flyers that described his educational and professional background; even if he was new to the Texas Republicans, he wanted to establish his political engagement from his days in Georgia. He also pursued another tactic by engaging in deep conversations with as many people as he could. Over the course of several days, Bill talked about his thoughts on Constitutionalism, liberty, and conservatism, making what he describes as "quite a few friends" in the process. He hoped that at the end of the day, people felt like they knew him and liked his convictions.

For his short speech, Bill focused on his experience as a professor, and on how he hoped to bring his political science students from South Texas College to the Electoral College vote in December to make the process come alive for them. "I explained that I was a strict Constitutionalist who believed in the Electoral College system, whereas most of my undergraduate students had never even heard of the Electoral College system before in their lives."

When the votes were tallied, Bill won in a surprise upset—by only two votes. "When I was chosen, I felt incredibly proud. It is a huge honor to be chosen as an elector. It's a position of great responsibility, and everyone who is chosen should feel truly honored."

The Corrupt Bargain

It was 1825, and Senator Andrew Jackson was furious. He penned a letter to his friend George Wilson, saying: "This, to my mind, is the most open, daring corruption that has ever shown itself under our government, and if not checked by the people, will lead to open direct bribery."

Eventually, Wilson's friendship with Jackson would be written as an interesting anecdote in several history books—recalling Wilson received (and rejected due to his personal moral objections) a presidential pardon from Jackson after having been sentenced to hanging after robbing a United States postal worker. However, that news would make waves in 1830. In 1825, George Wilson was still law-abiding, and Andrew Jackson was just considered a populist, rugged war hero. He was also a very jilted candidate in the 1824 presidential election, having lost what has now been termed "The Corrupt Bargain."

Since the tenuous 1800 election, in which Democratic-Republican Thomas Jefferson beat out Federalist John Adams, the Federalist Party was never able to regain its footing. When Hamilton, one of the nation's leading Federalists, died after a duel with Jefferson's Vice President, Aaron Burr, the party suffered a major blow. By the time of the War of 1812 with Great Britain, the Federalists had their last great push, which ultimately was unsuccessful. At the war's end, most of the major Federalists found their home within the Democratic-Republican Party and, for at least a time, it seemed like party politics might have been just a blip in the American political system. In the 1816 presidential election, Founding Father and former Secretary of State James Monroe easily beat out the Federalist candidate, eliciting 183 Electoral College votes, while New Yorker Rufus King won a mere 34.

With Monroe squarely in charge of the government, the Federalist Party disappeared. After the successful resolution of the War of 1812, it seemed like the less than 30-year-old country was on a course for smooth sailing. A Boston newspaper supposedly coined the term "the Era of Good Feelings," which quickly caught on. Of course, everything wasn't as peaceful as it might have appeared on the surface. Different regions of the country were faced with entirely different economic, social, and cultural circumstances. As the Founding Fathers had predicted at the 1787 Constitutional Convention, different regions favored their local political figures, most of whom lacked a wider national appeal. The divides between North and South, as well as westward expansion, contributed to factionalism.

When Monroe refused to name a successor at the end of his second term, perhaps he thought that it would help maintain stability. In fact, it had the opposite effect as four candidates quickly rose to the fore. They were Secretary of State John Quincy Adams, Speaker of the House Henry Clay, Secretary of the Treasury William Crawford, and Senator Andrew Jackson.

The heir apparent might have been embodied by John Quincy Adams. He was the son of Founding Father and former President John Adams and had a myriad of accomplishments under his belt, including serving as an ambassador in Europe, negotiating the Treaty of Ghent to end the War of 1812, and being an architect of the Monroe Doctrine, which denounced European involvement in the western hemisphere. He was an educated man of the enlightened Northeast: he was not only a lawyer, but also a professor at Harvard College. However, what he had in spades in credentials and intellectual capacity, he often lacked when it came to likeability and ability to navigate politics. To many of his peers, he came across as aloof and lacking the charm that it increasingly took to be elected President.

The United States had gone through tremendous changes. The population had grown substantially, from 3.9 million in 1790 to 9.6 million in 1820. Westward territories also changed the political and economic dynamics, shifting influence away from the southern slave-holding states. Additionally, although vastly insubstantial by today's standards, American politics were becoming increasingly democratic.

When it came to the Electoral College, more and more states were allowing citizens to choose their presidential electors directly. Of the twenty-four states in the country, three-fourths of them had developed a system based on the popular vote. Only in six states (Delaware, Georgia, Louisiana, New York, South Carolina, and Vermont) were electors chosen by state legislatures rather than by citizens. Thus, the election of 1824 would become the very first election that even measured the popular vote (although it should be viewed more as an indicator rather than a substantial metric, due to its exclusion of these six states.)

In spite of the increased role of citizens in the process, the system of electing a President did not resemble modern presidential elections. Instead of appealing to a mass public, potential candidates needed to get support from the electors, who were typically involved in some way in the electoral process. In *National Geographic*, journalist James Traub noted, "[Candidates] engaged in a ceaseless circuit of private talks with legislators and local power brokers. Candidates largely sat in one place and received reports from their friends, in person or by letter. Public address, either by candidates or their surrogates, were rare."

The antithesis of John Quincy Adams was also running for the 1824 presidency: a former general by the name of Andrew Jackson. While Adams grew up in a well-off, academic family, Andrew Jackson grew up in the rural frontier between North and South Carolina in a community of Scots-Irish. He never knew his father, who died before he was born, and was raised by his widowed mother. At the age of thirteen, he joined the militia in the American Revolution, which was more or less engaging in guerilla warfare tactics, alongside his brothers. One brother died of heatstroke in battle; another brother died of smallpox as a prisoner of war; and their mother tragically died from cholera after volunteering to nurse soldiers.

Like Adams, Jackson became a lawyer and he quickly rose to political fame in his adopted home: Nashville, in the new frontier state of Tennessee. He transitioned from politics to war in 1812. His escapades on the battlefield became the stuff of legends, written about nationwide. It started with the Battle of Horseshoe Bend, where United States forces defeated Creek Native Americans who opposed westward expansion in Alabama. Jackson then solidified his status as a war hero at the 1815 Battle of New Orleans, when American forces were able to fend off a British assault in

The 1824 Contingency Election

Era of Good Feelings
DEMOCRATIC-REPUBLICAN PARTY

John Quincy Adams
Secretary of State
Massachusetts

Henry Clay
Speaker of the House
Kentucky

William Crawford
Secretary of the Treasury
Georgia

Andrew Jackson
Senator
Tennessee

24 states voted in the 1824 election	In **3/4 of the states**, electors were selected by popular vote	In **1/4 of the states**, electors were selected by the state legislatures

1824 was the first election that counted popular vote as a metric

WITHOUT AN ELECTORAL COLLEGE MAJORITY WINNER, IT BECAME A CONTINGENCY ELECTION IN THE HOUSE OF THE REPRESENTATIVES

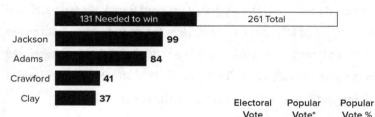

131 Needed to win	261 Total

Jackson **99**
Adams **84**
Crawford **41**
Clay **37**

	Electoral Vote	Popular Vote*	Popular Vote %
Adams	84	108,740	30.5
Clay	37	47,136	13.2
Crawford	41	46,618	13.1
Jackson	99	153,544	43.1

The only candidate with nationwide appeal, **Jackson** won an Electoral College **plurality** and the **popular vote**

*only counted in ¾ of the states

TOP 3
(Adams, Crawford, and Jackson)
As per the 12th Amendment, only the top three winners in the Electoral College were considered to the House of Representatives

FINAL RESULTS OF THE CONTINGENCY ELECTION
- Decided in the House of Representatives
- Each state got only one vote
- 13/24 states needed to win

 13 Adams
 7 Jackson
4 Crawford

WINNER
John Quincy Adams

the War of 1812, suffering only 250 casualties to Britain's 2,000 casualties, despite being outnumbered. Although the British were badly organized, it was nonetheless touted as a "miracle." Following New Orleans, Jackson was then sent to Florida, where he fought against the Seminole tribe. His military engagements provided precedent for Americans to enter Florida, which was then a Spanish territory. In 1819, Spain ceded Florida to the United States, after deciding that it could no longer afford to keep it garrisoned with soldiers.

If the presidency were a popularity contest in 1824, there is little doubt that Andrew Jackson probably would have won it, as his name had become a household one for his battlefield exploits. But, winning the presidency at the time was a more nuanced affair. For a while, it seemed like Georgia native William Crawford might have the lead, with tacit support from not one but two former Presidents: James Madison and Thomas Jefferson. However, at the time of the election, Crawford found himself paralyzed and nearly blind following a stroke. He went on to recover, returned to Georgia, and spent the rest of his days as a judge. But at the time, he refused to bow out of the race. Considering his physical situation, he still ended up doing pretty well, coming in third in the Electoral College.

Jackson got the most Electoral College votes, but still had only 99 out of the 131 needed to win the presidency. Adams received 84 Electoral College votes, while Crawford received 41 and Speaker of the House Henry Clay received 37. Perhaps unsurprisingly, the states had voted along regional lines for their "favored sons." Adams won in New England; Crawford won his home state of Georgia, as well as in Virginia and Delaware. Kentucky native Henry Clay won the western states, while Jackson won elsewhere, in part due to his widespread appeal. Jackson also won 41% of the popular vote (where it was counted); Adams came in second place with nearly 31% of the vote.

Andrew Jackson viewed himself as the winner of the contest, having achieved both the most popular votes and the most Electoral College votes. However, in the absence of a majority in the Electoral College, the Twelfth Amendment of the Constitution, signed into law a mere twenty years earlier, came into play, stipulating:

> *The person having the greatest number of votes for President, shall be the President, if such number be a majority of the whole number of Electors appointed; and if no person have such majority, then from the persons having the highest numbers not exceeding three on the list of those voted for as President, the House of Representatives shall choose immediately, by ballot, the President. But in choosing the President, the votes shall be taken by states, the representation from each state having one vote; a quorum for this purpose shall consist of a member or members from two-thirds of the states, and a majority of all the states shall be necessary to a choice.*

It was the first and only time in history since the passing of the Twelfth Amendment that a contingent election in the House of Representatives was required. As Henry Clay came in fourth, he was no longer a contender—only the top three candidates would be referred to the House of Representatives. However, scholars have noted that as Speaker of the House, Clay used this opportunity to play "kingmaker." Perhaps personal preferences led Clay to view Adams as a better choice for President than Jackson. He clearly did not think that Jackson was up for the job, saying, "I cannot believe that killing 2,500 Englishmen at New Orleans qualifies for the various, difficult, and complicated duties of the Chief Magistracy."

Regardless of the reason why, Clay had some of his friends reach out to Adams's camp. On a diary entry dated December 15, 1824, Adams wrote that a friend had come "and told me that he had it from good authority that Mr. Clay was much disposed to support me, if he could at the same time be useful to himself." On January 9, 1825, Clay and Adams met in private and spent the evening "in a long conversation."

It is unclear exactly what was said during that meeting, or if any agreement was made between the presidential candidate and the Speaker of the House. When the House of Representatives voted on February 9, 1825, Adams won exactly the 13 states he needed to win for the presidency. Jackson only won seven states, while Crawford won four. Perhaps the most suspicious for Adams's victory was the state of Kentucky, Clay's home state. Although Adams had not won a single vote in the state in the general contest, the Kentuckian quorum backed him for the presidency, despite the fact that Tennessee's Jackson had popular appeal in the state. Adams also won Ohio and Missouri, the two other states whose electors had voted for Henry Clay.

Jackson was shocked by the results, as was a large number of onlookers. Three days later, when Adams picked Clay as his Secretary of State, Jackson supporters cried foul. Jackson himself wrote in a letter to friend William Berkeley Lewis on February 14, 1825, "So you see, the Judas of the West [Clay] has closed the contract and will receive the thirty pieces of silver ... was there ever witnessed such a bare faced corruption in any country before?"

"The Corrupt Bargain" was certainly turned into a political rallying cry for Jackson's supporters, who believed that the election had been stolen from them. Jackson stated his intentions to run again for President four years later. Perhaps predicting the popular vote debate that rages in the country even today, abolishing the Electoral College and having the President directly elected by popular vote would become one of his platforms. At the time, Jackson had widespread populist appeal and would likely have done well in such contests. The divide between Jackson and Adams also re-established political parties. In 1828, Jackson ran as a Democratic candidate, while Adams ran as a National Republican candidate (a party which would soon become known as the Whigs).

Adams, like his father, would be relegated to being a one-term President, as he constantly faced opposition from Jackson supporters in the legislative branch. However, as damning as the facts may seem, there was never any formal investigation into the matter, and researchers have not been able to prove without a doubt that any "corrupt bargain" was actually entered into on the night Adams and Clay met. Perhaps Adams would have considered Clay for such a position even without an arrangement.

While this story may seem like far-flung history, it is worth noting that this was the last time that the Electoral College led to a contingent election, where the decision of who became President was determined in the House. While historical circumstances have not led to a repeat of the situation, the laws remain the same, with the Twelfth Amendment taking precedence in instances where the Electoral College does not have a majority victory. Even in modern times, a plurality of votes like in the case of Jackson's loss would likewise be determined in the House of Representatives by a quorum, each state with one vote, with the popular vote and Electoral College votes rendered obsolete.

Baoky Vu
Part 2

By late 2015, Baoky Vu had already jumped on the political train and was speeding straight ahead, putting all his efforts behind Jeb Bush's campaign in the Republican primary. Perhaps it came as no surprise to most, as Baoky previously had an appointment in George W. Bush's administration. Baoky appreciated and got along with the establishment, and Jeb was widely viewed as the establishment pick for the Republican primary—a former governor, a son of a former President, and the brother of a former President.

There were so many candidates in the field, though, that Baoky knew that it was going to be an exciting and wild ride. At the same time, he wasn't worried, as he surveyed the talented individuals who had put their hats in the ring for the Republican primary. "Most of us old business background politicos had shown our support for one candidate or another. We were against each other, but we all thought that one of our guys—Bush, Kasich, or Rubio—would come out on top," Baoky remembers. "We would all fall around the guy who won, no questions asked. We knew that one of them, and by default all of us, would come out okay." In his mind, there were no red flags or emergency signals that the traditional, establishment candidates wouldn't come out on top.

One candidate that Baoky was not concerned about at all was Donald Trump. When Trump had made his way down the New York City Trump Tower escalators to announce his candidacy, Baoky just shook his head in laughter. He didn't think for a second that Trump had any chance.

Sometime in February or March (he cannot remember exactly when), Baoky received a phone call saying that he had been nominated to be an elector in the Electoral College. "At the time I was only aware of the concept of the Electoral College," he admits. He had studied the Electoral College in school and knew all about the debate between the Electoral College and the national popular vote following the 2000 election, but he had "no idea about how the mechanisms of the Electoral College worked." However, he could tell by the way that it was presented to him that it was a big honor. He immediately began doing more research, and it dawned on him that he was being asked to partake in what he later described as "one of the nation's oldest historical institutions."

A week later, Baoky was at the Georgia State Capitol filling out a form with the other individuals nominated to be electors. Baoky discovered that all sixteen of them had been handpicked by the leadership of Georgia's Republican Party. He was quite surprised because he felt like he was an insider of sorts and he had never heard anyone talking about the Electoral College. In fact, he wasn't even entirely sure who had chosen him or why. Once all of the nominated electors filled out the form, each one of them had to pay what Baoky describes as a nominal fee ("only

$3 or something like that") and the form was submitted to the Georgia Secretary of State. After that, all of their names were in the history books; they were all official electors.

Baoky is unsure whether the Republican primaries had even taken place in Georgia by that time. Regardless, there was little indication of the tensions that would soon arise in the Republican Party as Trump began to surge against all the traditional candidates. Baoky believes that he was chosen as an elector because he had been a reliable and loyal member of the Party for quite literally decades. While you might see Tea Party people come and go, he was always there at events, supporting local, state, and national Republican candidates.

However, it was proving to be the most unusual of election years. "We started out with a Jeb Bush sign in our yard," Baoky remembers. "When Jeb dropped out, we switched out our Jeb sign to a Marco Rubio sign. After Rubio, we didn't know what to do." By the time the Republican National Convention came around, it was clear that Trump was the heir apparent. Even though Baoky didn't have any official business to attend to (he hadn't jumped on the bandwagon and started raising money for Trump), he traveled up to Cleveland for the RNC alongside his wife, who was an alternate delegate for Marco Rubio. He had been involved with the Georgia Republicans for so long that he knew that it would be a great time to catch up with friends across the country and enjoy the spectacle of the political convention.

Baoky describes himself as "fortunate" to have managed to attend a large number of RNCs. It all started in 1988 when he attended his first RNC in New Orleans, which he describes as "Reagan's farewell and Bush 41's rise." Baoky will never forget the fun he had as a college student, running around Bourbon Street with his young Republican university friends. "It was hot and muggy, but New Orleans was the place to be," he gushes. "During Reagan's farewell speech, there was not a dry eye in the Superdome. There was such a sense of 'Mission Accomplished,' an overwhelming feeling of the Reagan Revolution."

His palate for the RNC was whetted yet again in 2004, when he attended his second RNC as an alternate delegate for George W. Bush in New York City. Baoky also remembers that as a very positive convention, with former-Republican-turned-Democratic New York City mayor Michael Bloomberg giving a speech. "People were coming together," he recalls, "It was post 9/11 and people just weren't so angry with each other back then." In 2008, Baoky landed a place at the RNC in Minneapolis, where he was helping blog about the events for his hometown paper, the *Atlanta Journal-Constitution*. Although Baoky had originally been a supporter of Romney, he quickly got onto the McCain camp once the latter secured the nomination. He had nothing but respect for McCain's military service, noting that one of McCain's prisoner of war Hanoi Hilton cellmates, Orson Swindle, was a friend of the family.

By contrast, Baoky was finding the tone of Cleveland's RNC extremely dark. "I remember looking up and seeing [General] Michael Flynn on stage, who is this conspiracy theorist of sorts, shouting, 'Lock her up.' It just seemed in bad taste," he remembers. He wasn't going to let some negative messaging here and there ruin the fun with his wife and their Republican friends, though. As he recalls the RNC, he remembers how fun Cleveland was, having dinners which went late into the night by the Great Erie lake.

Baoky is pretty sure that he was not the only one who was uncomfortable with the tone that Trump's convention was taking. He remembers the rumors that were swirling around on the floor that there were plans to put Cruz or Kasich in Trump's place, although he lacks credible sources to confirm his suspicions. He left the day of Trump's acceptance speech, deciding that he would watch the highlights on the news, rather than seeing it live and in-person. "At the time, I was having mixed feelings about the guy," Baoky describes. "On the one hand, Trump was really entertaining to watch. I felt like he was BS-ing so much. It was like watching a half-comedy, half-reality show. There wasn't much substance to what he was saying."

When watching the highlights, however, Baoky was incredibly turned off by what he thought to be Trump's mean-spiritedness. He decided to himself that there was no way that Trump could win, as everyone was viewing him as a joke, so he started preparing himself for the inevitability of a Clinton presidency. As he began to think about it, he didn't think that it would end up being that bad of an administration. Baoky is a strong believer in the globalized economy. "I am a defender of Wall Street," he told me in an earlier conversation. "I think that capital markets are extremely efficient at allocating capital across the world. It does bring about unintended excess, but you have to appreciate how much capital it allocates to allowing economies and businesses to grow." In his mind, Bill Clinton's presidency in the 1990s did a lot to open up and grow the economy, so maybe a Clinton victory wouldn't be the worst thing in the world.

The weeks following the RNC and leading up to the DNC were a soul-searching time for Baoky and many other establishment Republicans. After Trump's "coronation," they were expecting him to lay off the right-wing rhetoric and become the Republican nominee they wanted him to be. When they realized that he was unwilling or unable to do that, people in the establishment circles began to whisper about whether they could support a man like that for President. They couldn't believe how he had been able to beat out so many of their conventional, establishment candidates.

"Who would have thought that I would be the one to do to something crazy?" Baoky asked during one of our conversations. I couldn't tell if his question was rhetorical, so I asked him to elaborate. He responded that he had always been the establishment guy, willing to follow the party line no matter what and follow rules by the book. He thinks that what transpired was ultimately out of character for him, although he doesn't regret having stood up for his beliefs.

As I pondered Baoky's case, I began to wonder if it was inevitable that Baoky would make such a moral grandstand, or if he was indeed triggered to do something so radical. Maybe Baoky would have done what he did regardless, or maybe it was truly Trump's response to the parents of Captain Humayun Khan that set him off. I began to wonder why this particular instance resonated so much with Baoky, rather than the plethora of Trump's other comments that had caused so much offense among others. Was it because Baoky, as a former refugee, felt some sort of kinship with this captain of Pakistani descent? Was it because Baoky understood how difficult it was for people of color to gain a foothold in the closed South? Was it because that when Trump made comments about Captain Humayun Khan, Baoky pictured his brother, who had served for five years as a naval cryptology officer, in his place? We will never know; perhaps Baoky doesn't even know himself.

What happened is that at the Democratic National Convention, Khizr and Ghazala Khan discussed the death of their son, a former ROTC student at the University of Virginia, who had been killed in an explosion in Iraq in 2004. Like Baoky, the Khans had previously been supporters of Ronald Reagan. However, they were so deeply upset by the comments of Donald Trump saying that he would ban Muslims from entering the country that they felt like they needed to speak out against it and remind the nation that Muslims were actively serving and dying for the United States. In a convention that was bitterly embroiled in disputes between the Clinton and Sanders delegates, the Khans' speech was widely regarded as one of the most powerful speeches of the entire convention.

Trump's response, in which he called the father emotional, suggested that the speech was written by the Clinton campaign, and claimed that the mother was silent because of conservative Islamic beliefs, caused outrage from both Democrats and Republicans. When Baoky heard Trump's comments, he found himself extremely angry. He also found himself in a moral conundrum. Baoky had been chosen by the Republican Party he cherished so much to vote for this man as President in the Electoral College. He knew that Georgia would probably go Republican for the election, which meant that he would be walled in to vote for Trump. What he was worried about was whether or not he could sign his name on the sheet of paper that would give Donald Trump the presidency directly.

Robert Satiacum
Part 1

On the last day of the Democratic National Convention, 56-year-old Robert Satiacum woke up early to walk around the city of Philadelphia. While walking its empty streets at 5:30 A.M., he imagined how hundreds of years ago, the Founders had been engaged in the American Revolution. "Everywhere I looked was bricks, stones, glass, and concrete," recounts Robert. "I thought to myself that the black and white eagle feather, the leather bag of cedar chips, and the drum I was carrying were actually the only real things in the entire place. They were the only things that had come from the earth."

It was a disconcerting end to a disconcerting trip. But even before the 2016 election cycle, Robert felt an intense sense of dysfunction in society. "My heart was breaking," he remembers. A member of the Puyallup tribe in the northwest of Washington state, Robert had started to get more active with pan-indigenous topics since starting his own radio talk show, which often featured guests from around the country. For one hour at noon on Thursdays, Robert would take the reins from what he describes as a traditional, white, and over-60 radio station for his own "Tribal Talk Radio" to discuss issues associated with indigenous peoples and communities.

Robert clearly loved his radio show, describing in detail how he carefully managed the one hour slot to provide listeners with a holistic experience, in which people not only learned about social ills, but also felt as if they could end up making a difference. He tried to accomplish this through his unique style of accepting all of his listeners and guests as family, infusing the radio show with prayers to the creator, as well as explanations of his philosophy about the earth, water, air, and oxygen. While the work could often lead him to feel depressed, it also made him keenly aware of many issues facing Native American communities. At first, he wanted to run it like a "sweat lodge," where people could just talk about different issues, but once atrocities started occurring—"a dam here; a dam there; oil in the river"—Robert knew that he had to expand the scope of his show.

These experiences made Robert interested in the Bernie Sanders campaign, not because of what Sanders promised to do, but simply because he was willing to listen. "He reached out to our native communities and people told him our struggles," Robert remembers. "We told him about the pipeline—and about the copper mines and gold mines that were being dug on our sacred land. He listened."

Even though Sanders had gained traction, Robert claims that everybody in political circles inherently understood that Hillary Clinton was going to be "the next one to ascend to the throne." Although he claims that he was relatively quiet about his frustration, a turning point for him was when his tribe, along with another 29 tribes in Washington state, gave

Clinton hundreds of thousands of dollars in donations. "It was a weaving conference or a women's conference or something like that early on in the campaign," Robert says. "Basically, she just wanted a photo op with all of these native people. The photos and the headlines felt like a lie, especially when Bernie started really taking the time to understand our troubles."

Robert grew up in a family deeply involved in tribal politics. Although his father is remembered as a relatively controversial figure (the first American Indian to seek and be granted refugee status in Canada after being convicted in the United States for the embezzlement of tribal funds), like many a son who respects his father, Robert talks exclusively about the positive changes his father brought about for the community. "We used to be so poor. My grandmother sent my dad and uncles to the train tracks, so that they could grab the corn and grains that happened to fall off the train for dinner," Robert says impassionedly. In 1954, his father (Robert Satiacum, Sr.) was arrested for illegally fishing in the Puyallup River, and started a campaign among his tribe for the native residents to demand fishing rights. The movement gained more and more popularity, to the point that Hollywood heartthrob Marlon Brando was arrested alongside Robert Sr. during one of his so-called "fish-ins."

His father was intent on establishing new revenue streams for the tribal members, empowering people to make a better life for themselves by starting their own businesses to sell tax-free cigarettes, liquor, and fireworks. Eventually taking on the role of Chairman of the Tribe, Robert Sr. was instrumental in building a much-needed, profit-generating casino. With his fame spread across indigenous communities, he was bestowed the title of "chief of chiefs of all nations."

"Our tribal council started very humbly. It was 1970, and a lot of people just met up in my auntie's laundry room," Robert now laughs. Even though tribal politics seemed like second nature to Robert, he claims that national and state politics were something that he never engaged in much as a young man. "Growing up, I always thought I was Republican," he claims. "I didn't even pick up voting until I was older. I wasn't taught about politics and elections in school, and when election time came, it didn't seem very important."

The elections of 2006 and 2008 really impacted Robert, who began to believe that "state politicians were trying to use our tribe for their own benefit; just coming around when they wanted donations." In 2009, everything changed for Robert when he decided that he wanted to restore the original sacred name of Washington's Mount Rainier: Ti'Swaq.

"The mountain has been named after a person, which to us, is not accurate. The mountain is something sacred and holy," Robert describes as his initial motivation. He decided to organize the Day of 1,000 Drums and call on Native Americans and activists from outside Tacoma to bring national attention to the issue. "At first, I just wanted to teach people that this beautiful mountain has a feeling, that it has a heart." At the Day of 1,000 Drums, Robert remembers that he met a nature guy who was there to register voters. After a short conversation, Robert claims that they decided that they should start a campaign for the Washington Democrats to include the renaming of Mt. Rainier into the state party platform. This is how Robert remembers that he became an active Democrat.

By 2010, Mt. Rainier's renaming had been introduced as a House Bill. "I got absorbed in it. My ego was getting fed," remembers Robert, who became the head of his caucus. His wife of over twenty years, Elizabeth, also was active in politics alongside him, becoming a delegate and an elector in 2012 for the Democratic Party. "It was like I had been given a cape that had a big 'S' on my chest for 'Super Indian.' I was out there to change the system. But all of that changed with the DNC [in 2016]. Between Friday and Sunday, I had decided that I was done with politics forever. If Sanders had quit fighting, it meant that he was just like all of the other politicians."

Robert had told his political friends beforehand that he didn't even want to go to Philadelphia, if it meant that all he was going to see was Clinton win. He remembers being told that Sanders supporters were not planning on giving up so easily, and that they needed people like himself there at the convention if everything was going to go according to their plan. Robert wasn't sure what the plan was, but for sure, he didn't want to be the one to mess it up. The whole time in Philadelphia, Robert claims that he was uncomfortable: he didn't like seeing the police and the SWAT teams set up all over the city. He didn't like seeing news cameras all over the place just to discover that when he flipped on the news to MSNBC, he didn't see any footage that resembled what he was actually experiencing.

On Saturday morning, Robert met with some of his buddies from tribes in other states to attend Bernie's speech. The night before, he remembers how everyone had been drinking, celebrating, and calculating what needed to be done to secure Sanders's nomination. Likening it to waiting in line for a rock concert, Robert recalls the pins-and-needles anticipation. "This was the reason that we got on the flights to Philadelphia to start with," he comments. "We were all Bernie delegates and we didn't believe it was over." When Bernie took the stage, the auditorium erupted in triumphant cheers.

As Bernie began to talk, Robert could hear a pin drop. When it became apparent that Sanders intended to reiterate that he had conceded the nomination to Clinton, the mood suddenly changed. "Everyone in that auditorium was having a 'what the F' moment," Robert remembers looking at the people surrounding him wearing green Robin Hood hats, who seemed like they were going into shock. He heard a woman cry out from the side, "Why, Bernie, why?" and things began to go crazy. Robert's memory includes people yelling and screaming and throwing things into the air. In that one moment, Robert had a feeling of dread: that everything was going to go haywire, and the reason for all of the police and cameras was to cover up the dirty work behind the scenes.

"I look back at the tapes of the DNC and I wonder if I saw things wrongly, if I was just making stuff up in my head, or imagining things, because what I see I don't remember happening," Robert claims of the formal nomination of Clinton later that day. "I truly don't remember anything but echoes of frustration inside of that Wells Fargo Center." He didn't feel the need to stick around to hear "that horrible sentence" proclaiming Clinton as the nominee. Along with "hundreds of Bernie supporters," he went into the media tent in an effort to make the truth known. Followed in by police, Robert describes their stint in the media tent almost like imprisonment. Without food or water, they sat and waited for hours. Some people were so upset that they put tape over their mouths. Robert, however, refused to be silent. I later managed to find several YouTube videos, including Robert's impassioned speeches from the media tent, floating out there on the internet.

He was one of the last ones to leave the media tent. "Everyone should have known that there was no way that Bernie delegates were going to join Clinton's ranks," Robert claims. He remembers delegates leaving, one-by-one, typically to drown their sorrows in alcohol at their hotels. Others decided that they would rather join Jill Stein than back Hillary Clinton. He recounts bits and pieces of the DNC with fervor, jumping back and forth between days and topics, later claiming that he feels as if he had developed PTSD from the experience.

But Robert felt a level of empowerment that many delegates did not: he knew that at the end of the day, he still had a say in the final election—not the election in November, but the election in December with the

Electoral College. He is still a bit hazy on the details of how he was chosen as an elector at the Washington State Democrat Convention. "Everyone knew I was a Bernie guy," he claims, not knowing why he would be suggested as an elector to begin with.

A part of his haziness in the details is due to the chaos associated with the Convention itself. The Nevada and Utah Democratic State Conventions had just taken place, and the Clinton-Sanders divide was evident in those two arenas. According to Robert, his local convention had likewise quickly disintegrated into chaos. He only remembers a couple of Clinton supporters, claiming that the rest were clearly in the Sanders camp. Regardless, there was enough arguing to make sure that nothing was getting done. The two sides were resisting each other, going back and forth.

Robert was passing the time, talking to a woman sitting next to him. When it came time to fill the elector positions still available, he claims that he heard a voice calling out that he had been nominated as an elector. His first thought was that of frustration, wondering who would have possibly put him on the list. He had been approached by some of his political contacts in 2012 to become an elector and when he said that he wasn't interested, his wife Elizabeth had jumped at the chance. He proudly told me that his wife was one of the first Native American women to vote for Barack Obama in the Electoral College.

Looking around to find the culprit, he realized that one of his elders had nominated him. At that singular moment, Robert was conflicted. "I wanted to say no; I didn't want that role. I was getting my legs together to stand up and walk to the microphone and say that," he recalls. "But something inside of me told me that I couldn't just say no. She was my elder. To make society run smoothly, you can't just go against your elders." As Robert pondered simultaneously a rejection and an acceptance speech, he saw a young man stand up and rush to the microphone to give his own speech. Before he knew it, he claims, the whole ceremony just progressed, moving on to one person and then the next.

At some point, he just decided to slip out. He thought that maybe he would have a chance to talk once things died down. But by the time he got back, the line was even longer; everyone was lining up to give speeches to be chosen as an elector. So, he left again to get a hamburger. "Those shenanigans were going on for hours," he claims, "When I got back, the next thing I knew was that people were congratulating me and I was getting voted in. I just kept thinking to myself what was going on, because I hadn't given a speech. I hadn't even accepted the nomination. But everybody was smiling and patting me on the shoulder." Robert walked out of the state convention with one of his elders, who turned to him with a big smile, commenting that Robert was pretty popular. He had gotten 1,379 votes. It was the first time that Robert had heard that number.

At the DNC, it dawned on Robert that he could just end up voting for Sanders regardless. But after seeing Sanders give up at the DNC, he was beginning to question that. "When Bernie said that we should vote for Hillary instead of voting for him, it upset me. I wondered: why should I vote for him, if he didn't even want me to?" The whole political process felt to Robert "like a scripted joke."

Perhaps Robert was similarly impacted by his upbringing. To him, the convention was just one more example of a modern culture that is increasingly restrictive. "Everyone is just focused on being the winner. People are telling their children that they need to grow up to be winners, too. They believe that you have to hurt other people in order to get what you want. I don't believe in that. I want to be a holy man."

He described the rest of his 2016 summer as uneventful and filled with quiet resignation. "I have been in addiction recovery for twenty years. I realize that I am on borrowed time. I just wanted to leave politics behind me, go home, and make peace with my maker in this time that I have left," Robert comments. Filled with the desire to put his family first, he went home to Tacoma to enjoy time with his five children, 11 grandchildren, and one great-grandchild. The Electoral College vote was still a long way away, and to be honest, he just didn't want to think about it until then.

The Libertarian

When he was a wide-eyed teenager, Roger MacBride met Rose Wilder Lane for the first time. It was during World War II, and his father, an editor for *Reader's Digest*, was working to shorten one of her works for publication. Rose was forty-something years Roger's senior and was something of a legend. For the last two decades, she had established herself as one of America's top best-selling and well-paid female writers; her works were in a surprising array of publications, from *Harper's* to *Good Housekeeping*, from *Cosmopolitan* to *Ladies' Home Journal*.

Rose was not only prolific, but also incredibly interesting. Her childhood was something that storybooks were made of—quite literally. She was the only surviving child of prolific "rugged pioneer" novelist Laura Ingalls Wilder, who based her manuscripts on events from her own life settling in America's newly acquired western territories between 1870 and

1894. (In fact, historians have debated the meteoric rise of Laura Ingalls Wilder, suggesting that Rose may have played a significant role in editing or even ghost-writing the beloved children's adventure stories.)

Besides her family pedigree, Rose was a unique character in her own right, constantly bucking traditional societal conventions. By the end of World War I, she was a childless divorcee, sustaining her own writing and editing career, and living what some people referred to as a "nomadic" lifestyle. It was then that she took a journalism assignment from the American Red Cross Publicity Bureau to write about war-torn Europe.

Although she was a supporter of communism, a conversation with a farmer from Georgia while on assignment made her start questioning the Soviet dream and economic model. She later wrote about her encounters in-depth, saying, "I came out of the Soviet Union no longer a communist because I believed in personal freedom. Like all Americans, I took for granted the individual liberty to which I had been born. It seemed as necessary and as inevitable as the air I breathed."

After her return to the United States (which coincided with her near pennilessness following the 1929 stock market crash), Rose became increasingly political, especially as a critic of Franklin Delano Roosevelt's "New Deal" stimulus. Over the coming decades, her fame rose with her dramatic political comments. (She once refused to accept a social security number, claiming that it reminded her of Nazi Germany: "I will have nothing to do with that Ponzi fraud because it is treason . . . I won't have it; you can't make me.")

By all accounts, Roger was mesmerized by Rose, who took a special interest in him. A podcast from the conservative Mises Institute describes their relationship as "devoted friends . . . Within a couple of years, he was calling her 'Gramma' and coming to spend weekends with her, weeding her garden, running her errands, and talking with her about history, economics, politics, and philosophy." He got a boost early in his career by managing her finances (which had grown significantly with the ongoing popularity of her mother's books). When she passed away in 1968, she named Roger as her sole heir and executor.

It was a windfall for the thirty-nine-year-old lawyer, described as akin to winning the lottery. But as a young man, Roger clearly didn't take his adopted grandmother's resources or attention for granted, establishing himself in his own right via his many academic and professional successes. He consistently pushed himself, first at New Hampshire's prestigious Phillips Exeter Academy, and then at Princeton as an undergraduate and Harvard as a law student. After graduating in 1951, he went to the Philippines as a Fulbright Scholar to study comparative constitutional systems. He then started a career at a Wall Street law firm before setting up a base in Virginia, where he managed Rose's affairs.

When Rose passed away, Roger sought to memorialize her legacy, eventually selling a family-friendly western television program to NBC based on the "Little House" books. Indeed, because of Roger's tenacity, the books' descriptions of the rugged Minnesota frontier captured the imagination of a generation of youngsters throughout the 1970s and 1980s.

Perhaps most importantly, Roger was a devoted ideological disciple of Rose Wilder Lane, who is now considered alongside Ayn Rand and Isabel Paterson as one of the mothers of modern libertarianism. Rose's political guidance likely started when he was still a young man, as evidenced through his political writings that focused on individual empowerment. In 1953, Roger wrote an 89-page treatise, *The American Electoral College*, espousing his beliefs on the Constitution's original intention, lamenting "mechanical men" and "electors [who] almost never exercise independent judgement." Analyzing James Madison's works, Roger argued for a "district" system of voting for electors.

His idea was clearly innovative for its time. Both Maine and Nebraska have since adopted this "district" system. (In today's modern political climate, these two states are most often referred to as the states that do not have a "winner-take-all" system.) In most states, all the state electors will vote for the winner of their state's popular general election, regardless of whether the margin is 0.1% or 10%. By contrast, in Maine and Nebraska, two electors are assigned to vote for the winner of the statewide popular vote (just as two senators represent the entire population.) Then, the vote is divided by congressional district; electors are expected to vote for the winner of the popular election of their respective districts—which has led to historically interesting results.

In 2008, Barack Obama won the popular vote of Nebraska's 2nd Congressional District, garnering him an Electoral College vote in a predominantly red state. Likewise, in 2016, Donald Trump was able to finagle a victory in Maine's 2nd Congressional District, giving him a red vote in the overwhelming Democratic Northeast. However, what Roger was most likely thinking when he first proposed the "district" system was how it might make it easier for independent candidates to make inroads into the two-party duopoly.

His writings on the Electoral College were clearly largely forgotten, or else he probably would not have been selected as an elector by Virginia's Republican Party in 1972. In hindsight, the 1972 election would go down in history as Nixon's downfall; his team wiretapped the Democratic National Committee's headquarters at the Watergate Hotel in Washington, D.C. When the scandal broke, Nixon faced impeachment from the House of Representatives and resigned days later on August 9, 1974. His running mate, Spiro Agnew, had resigned from the vice-presidency over a year earlier, after allegations of bribery and tax fraud, and was replaced on October 10, 1973 by Gerald Ford. After Nixon's resignation, Ford would become the 38th President of the United States—the first (and only) "unelected President" in the nation's history because of his absence on the 1972 ballot.

Looking at the election statistics, however, it is difficult to imagine that the Nixon/Agnew ticket would have faced so much resistance. The Democratic challenger, George McGovern, won in only 130 of some 3,100 counties across the entire United States, not even winning a majority in his home state of South Dakota. Also, McGovern won only 17 out of the 538 Electoral College votes. There were only small pockets of political resistance against the Nixon presidency, including the Libertarian Party, which was established in June of 1972, in part to protest Nixon's wage and price controls.

However, the Libertarian Party did not get off to a strong footing, and by the time of the presidential election a few months later, it had managed to secure its place on the ballots of only two states. The party's presidential ticket received a paltry 3,673 votes nationwide. At the time, it seemed like the fledgling Libertarian Party would meet the fate of so many other smaller political parties of the era—a slow and painful death. In fact, many third parties placed far ahead of the Libertarian Party: the American Independent Party got 1.1 million votes in 1972, while the Social Workers, People's, and Socialist Labor Party got more than 50,000 votes each. But the Libertarian Party had a trick up its sleeve: a Libertarian sympathizer and Rose's ideological heir, who was deeply entrenched inside Virginia's local Republican party.

We can only imagine how when the votes were tallied, Virginia politicos must have been shocked to hear of votes for John Hospers as President and Theodora Nathan as Vice President. It is likely that they wouldn't even have known who these individuals were, as the Libertarian Party had not been listed on the Virginia ballot.

Such a deviation from party politics was indeed shocking. MacBride later told reporters that he switched his vote to Hospers and Nathan "on behalf of the millions in this country who have helplessly watched the President inexorably move the federal government in the direction of ever greater control over the lives of all of us." Many papers didn't know how to respond to this seemingly outright insubordination, with the *Roanoke Times* trying to smooth things over. They ended their article with platitudes for the President-elect Nixon, claiming that Roger believed Nixon was "a thoughtful, intelligent man who is motivated by a sincere wish to do the best he can for his country."

However, from an historical standpoint, Roger's vote was legendary. His chosen presidential candidate, John Hospers, the philosophy chair at the University of Southern California, is often considered the first openly gay man to run for President. (While some say that Hospers had not come out in the modern sense of the term, others says that he was as open about his sexual orientation as he could be in 1972.) Hospers remains the first and only openly gay man to have received an actual Electoral College vote for President.

Hospers's running mate, journalist Theodora "Tonie" Nathan was both Jewish and a woman; Roger's vote for her has been memorialized in history as the first Electoral College vote for a woman, as well as for a Jewish individual. Additionally, in one fell swoop, with MacBride's vote, the Libertarian Party was on its way to becoming the third most important political party in the entire country due to a faithless elector.

By 1976, it seemed like Roger was becoming a major political figure in his own right, chosen as the Libertarian Party's nominee for President. Some have slyly noted that the Wilder fortune and the ability to finance his own campaign may have been a much more compelling reason for Roger's nomination than his policies. For the 1976 election, he flew across the country on his private propeller-driven plane, making plans from "an office that once was the slave kitchen of his 166-year-old mansion in Esmont, Virginia." Rumored to have been designed by none other than Thomas Jefferson himself, *People Magazine* noted, tongue-in-cheek, "From its long, white-columned porch, MacBride can look out over his herd of black Angus cattle and contemplate the millennium of diminished government." While MacBride didn't have a good shot at winning the presidency, he established a foothold for the nascent party, and notably elicited 5.5% of the popular vote in the state of Alaska.

Roger's 1976 campaign caught the attention and the monetary support of the late David Koch (one of the infamous, conservative-movement-financing Koch Brothers of Jane Mayer's *Dark Money* fame). The Koch Brothers had even deeper ties to Roger that bordered on the familial: both Charles and David Koch attended the Freedom School in Colorado, a free-market academy supported by Rose Wilder Lane with the growing fortune from her mother's books.

After MacBride's failed 1976 campaign for President, the Koch Brothers began to turn toward the Republican Party to meet their political ambitions. Roger resisted this strategy for a while, but by the early 1990s, he had also reverted to his Republican roots. He chaired the Republican Liberty Caucus until his death from heart failure at his home in Miami Beach in 1995. With his Libertarian legacy tainted by his flip to the Republicans, and his Republican legacy tainted by his faithless vote against Nixon, Roger's legacy and renegade spirit are exemplified that in one single vote, with which he pioneered not one but three firsts for the Electoral College.

Baoky Vu
Part 3

Baoky Vu woke up with a start at 4 A.M. at his home in Decatur, Georgia, in early August 2016, thinking to himself, "I just cannot do this anymore." He now describes himself as having felt like he had been pushed to the brink. He had taken great offense at how Trump had treated the parents of Captain Humayun Khan after the Democratic National Convention. Every day, Donald Trump seemed to say something new and outrageous. "There were values of mine that Trump breached and very specific ways in which he had breached them," Baoky comments. He wanted to make his stand by writing an op-ed for his local paper, the *Atlanta Journal-Constitution*. He wanted Georgians to know that there were many locals within the Republican Party who did not agree with Donald Trump as the nominee.

Over the years, Baoky had written op-eds for the *Atlanta Journal-Constitution*; he had even blogged for them during the 2008 Republican National Convention in Minneapolis. Even though Baoky keeps his television watching to a minimum, he views political messaging as a personal hobby. He remembers following his dad around as the latter gave speeches in Australia, trying to drum up support for the displaced South Vietnamese government. As a younger man, he loved listening to and reading speeches from known orators. Besides his beloved Ronald Reagan, another one of his favorites was Winston Churchill. He sat down and began to craft a message that he thought might resonate with his fellow Georgians.

Remembering that there were many Republicans on the national stage beginning to speak out against Trump, including foreign policy and national security hands, Baoky thought it might be nice for people to read an op-ed from a local perspective. Looking back on what happened, he assures me, "I wasn't trying to be a political capitalist. When I wrote it, I actually didn't expect that it would get any traction outside of the state at all. I think Mitt Romney had started calling him out. I thought that there was no way that people would be more interested in what I had to say than what Mitt Romney had to say."

The main difference is that Baoky was an Electoral College elector for the state of Georgia; Mitt Romney was not. When Baoky suggested that he would not vote for Donald Trump as an elector in his op-ed, he admittedly hadn't done the research; he didn't exactly know what it might mean from a legal or political perspective. He was just writing something that he felt was authentic and written from the heart. "It was a short statement—less than 350 words," he remembers. "I didn't feel like it needed to be much longer than that to get the point across." He reviewed it one more time for edits before sending it off to a friend at the local paper:

I've been active in the Republican Party for many years precisely because it has championed the aspirational ideals of Lincoln, Reagan and Kemp. Our recent standard-bearers have proudly and honorably defended those ideas on the political battlefield. From Bush 41 to Romney to Jeb and many of the other 2016 primary contestants, there was never a wavering doubt as to their character, integrity and temperament.

Until now.

This is the Republican Party of Lincoln and Reagan and Romney and Ryan, not the Party of Donald Trump. As a 2016 Presidential Elector, I am forever grateful to our state Party and our Chairman for bestowing this once-in-a-lifetime honor on me. I take my role seriously and in the face of the difficult choice before us, I will always put America First over party and labels.

Thus, I will not be voting for Donald Trump in the general election. My conscience is clear but my soul is being tested. Born in Saigon, my family knows what it is like to lose a country and my family is forever indebted to America and our allies. I have never questioned the soul, character and goodness of the Nation by who we have chosen as our leader throughout history.

Until now.

Rather than earning the American people's respect and trust through the duration of the past year, Donald Trump's antics and asinine behavior cemented my belief that he lacks the judgment, temperament and gravitas to lead this Nation. Throughout the process, he has hurled insults at our heroes and their families, denigrated the disabled and praised dictators. Forget political incorrectness, this is simply despicable demagoguery.

In this time of global challenges, we will succeed only if we come

*together. We've done it before, from the courthouse steps of Appomattox
to the days after Pearl Harbor. And to my Republican brothers and
sisters in arms, politics should be an honorable sport. Rather than fighting to defend the indefensible, let's live to fight another day.*

When Baoky was contacted by *Atlanta Journal-Constitution* columnist
Jim Galloway, he was surprised by the tone of the conversation—something along the lines of, "Are you really sure that you want to put this
out there?" Galloway mentioned the practical and political implications
it might have on Baoky, as well as his wife, who was also in the political
sphere. Baoky considered this and asked for his wife's name and profession
not to be mentioned in the op-ed. This was his thing, not hers. Galloway mentioned that as the statement was so short, he would write up an
accompanying article to contextualize it. Perhaps most interesting (and
startling to readers), Galloway mentioned in his accompanying article
that Georgia was one of the then 21 states where electors are unbound
and not required from any legal perspective to vote for the candidate who
won the state's popular vote.

It ended up being a powerful article, with Galloway quoting Baoky
that when fleeing Saigon, his family "hungered for the right to vote. I'm
not going to throw that away." Once again, Galloway asked if Baoky was
fine with going public. Baoky remembers being surprised at the comment.
"I was wondering why he kept asking that question. He writes a new blog
post about Georgia politics every day. I didn't understand how this might
be any different."

Little did Baoky know the reaction that the blog post would garner
once Jim sent it out to *Newswire*. "It went absolutely crazy," Baoky comments. He remembers seeing his name trending on AOL, Google, and
Yahoo. His phone was blowing up with messages; everyone from his

Georgetown network was sending it around. People in his largely liberal Decatur neighborhood were starting to come up to him and give him hugs. Democrats and progressives from across the country were writing to Baoky, calling him a "hero" for standing up to Trump. This sort of praise made Baoky extremely uncomfortable. "I don't think I am a hero by any stretch of the imagination. There are so many people who have made the ultimate sacrifice by fighting for their country. I responded by saying that those people are the true heroes, not me."

Baoky believes that the timing of his letter is what made it so poignant. It was long before Trump would end up winning the election and many, like himself, thought that Trump did not have much of a shot at winning, regardless of how Baoky voted. Instead, he says that his letter made people question a system that they had come to take for granted. "We hadn't had a faithless elector in many years and the Electoral College had become a de facto event. People were so comfortable with the Electoral College that they didn't think about the mechanisms of how it worked," Baoky comments. "When they read my statement, they began to think about what would happen if you started to have electors who would go against the grain. Here in Georgia, I was considered a heretic."

Baoky had been careful not to share his statement with any of his friends in the GOP beforehand. He didn't think that it would be right to force them to carry his burden. He also thought, in case there was pressure from the higher-ups, that he would rather his friends in the GOP be able to say that they were blindsided by his statement, rather than feign ignorance or the possibility of looking complicit if they admitted that they knew beforehand. When one of the state Republican leaders called him, they had a long conversation to determine how it might play out. They decided to see what sort of reaction the article might garner throughout the day.

Baoky's letter was already getting a lot of response. Baoky previously had his run-ins with the Georgia Tea Party movement, but it seemed like the entire wrath of the movement was upon him when Galloway quoted Tea Party activist Debbie Dooley saying, "[he] is a disgrace and Republicans should be outraged over Vu's stance to help Hillary. It is an embarrassment to the Georgia Republican Party." Referring to them as the "crazy crowd" who would support Trump no matter what he said or did, Baoky claims that he tried to address as many of them as he could respectfully, because he knew that they were upset. "In a political world, I have had to develop a thick hide, which helped me in this case," he remembers. He tried not to pay attention to many of the negative comments on the internet that were being written about him, but when he started to receive death threats and read comments by bloggers that he should be deported back to Vietnam, he felt increasingly concerned.

The one demographic that he was not prepared to be so upset were his parents. "My parents and all of their Vietnamese friends thought that I had gone completely off the rails when I wrote that letter," Baoky comments. "My father was actually quite upset when he saw the news. I think that most Vietnamese in that generation felt like they had been abandoned by the Democratic Party and needed to support the Republicans no matter what." Many of Baoky's friends were also surprised that he had done something like this, even though they weren't necessarily upset about it. He was supposed to be the poster child of the Republican establishment, with a refugee background story to boot. They were surprised that he was willing to possibly give it all up.

By the end of the day, Baoky had been contacted by local as well as international news outlets like CNN asking for comment on his letter. Friends from all over the world had messaged to share their opinions and ideas. To Baoky, there were only a few opinions that mattered still: all of them were in the Georgia Republican leadership. "We had a phone call at the end of the day," Baoky remembers. "It was evident that this thing was no longer self-contained. The most important thing for me was that I would be able to continue working with the local and state Republican candidates that I was helping out. I didn't want to alienate any of my friends or hurt their political futures."

Baoky also knew that he was still an appointed member on a couple of boards; he didn't want to create waves when it came to working with other Republicans in the future. Baoky offered to step down or to be removed as an elector, depending on what the Republican Party leadership thought was best. After some discussion, it was decided that Baoky would step down. "In this era, everything happens so fast with communication and technology. I didn't fully appreciate it until after it happened," Baoky comments.

He was told that the State Counsel for the Georgia Republican Party would soon be in contact to discuss procedures on how to step down officially. A couple of weeks later, Baoky was contacted that there was no official process to step down and they were unsure legally how to do it. It was ultimately decided that Baoky simply would not show up for the vote on December 19. When his name would be called for his signature, he would be unable to come up and do that. The Republican Party would have someone in the wings, willing and able to immediately take his place. It wasn't a perfect solution; but they decided that this was the best that they could do.

For Baoky, it was just one more interesting fact about the Electoral College, which he began to explore even more after the fact, as he considered the legal implications of what he did. Since he had written the letter, his neighbors and friends were constantly coming up to him, asking about his experience with the Electoral College and how he was chosen to be an elector in the first place. Baoky did additional research and even went through The Federalist Papers with the dean of the Georgia State Honors College. He began to consider the intention of the Electoral College, which is something that he had never thought of before. "I think the intent of the Founders was to provide a check and balance to the system with the Electoral College. That is why smaller states can have more of an influence; they can check the larger states. I want the Electoral College to be kept, but so many states have changed the rules to force you to vote for their candidate," Baoky comments, after having done the research after his historic letter. "The states effectively muted the original checks-and-balances intent."

Although he got several letters asking him if he would still stay on as an elector to vote against Trump, Baoky did not change his mind. From his perspective, he had already said what he needed to say. He wanted to continue supporting his friends in the Republican Party (although he now notes that he is more selective about which candidates he decides to assist). The letters did move him, however, as they reminded him of what he describes as "America's amazing political culture and process." When December 19 came, Baoky stayed home. Some of his friends (who were also in the Electoral College) messaged him and said that they still wished that they could have been electors together.

Baoky continues to remember the number of people who would come up to him at Republican events after the election, saying that they were inspired by and supported the stand that he decided to make against Trump. These instances inspire Baoky, who comments, "If you came out against Trump, you now have no hope of participating in GOP politics on the national scale. There are no places for people like me. Some Republicans, frustrated with the whole thing, just decided to switch parties and become Democrats. And then there are the ones like me: we are in touch with each other, waiting and hoping that things will start to change."

Although he is disillusioned with the Republican Party, he doesn't see a better place for himself to fit in. As we end one of our conversations, he comments wistfully, "Sometimes I wonder if I am a member of a silent majority inside my own party. Maybe both parties have their own silent majorities, whose voices aren't being heard at this time."

Robert Satiacum
Part 2

It was Halloween night of 2016, and Robert Satiacum was feeling a bit uneasy. "On Halloween, you have all of this bullshit going on. You have vampires and ghosts and Frankenstein. And here we are acting like all of this is normal. And I felt this voice, deep inside of me, saying, 'Go home. To the people. Go to where it all makes sense.'"

Robert told his wife, Elizabeth, that he thought that they needed to go to Standing Rock in South Dakota. She immediately understood and after the very last trick-or-treat candy was passed out, she told their son, Sonny Boy, that it was time to get in the car: that they were going to Standing Rock to join in the protests against the underground Dakota Access Pipeline, which cut through ancient indigenous burial grounds and had the potential to contaminate the local water supply.

After the Philadelphia DNC fiasco, Robert had been doing a lot of soul searching. One day, he had a vision: he felt like he was being called to create a global human necklace, a chain reaction of people encouraging each other to live peacefully with Mother Nature by focusing on the purity of water. "Today, nobody asks how we kept ancient forests alive for so many years. Today, we are destroying what is ancient—the ancient waters, the ancient streams. We don't focus on the spiritual nature of things anymore." The very next day, he saw the news about the dogs of law enforcement attacking the pacific Standing Rock protestors. Robert was sure that somehow the two were connected, and he had a deep desire to share his vision with Faith Spotted Eagle.

Faith had been a guest on Robert's Tribal Talk Radio show a couple of times for subjects like the Keystone XL Pipeline and the Nebraska Alliance. With all of their mutual friends, Robert felt a closeness to her and respected her work on Standing Rock in which she was described as a "principled moral leader." Robert had considered going to Standing Rock several times but was worried about whether or not he should bring his family along. He decided that this was the right opportunity to teach Sonny Boy about his heritage, even though it would be a long journey across Washington and Montana. They left in the middle of the night.

To help teach Sonny Boy, they stopped at the site of Custer's Last Stand (also known as the Battle of the Little Bighorn of 1876) in Montana. It was an overwhelming victory for the Lakota Sioux and the Northern Cheyenne tribes against the United States government as they sought to retain control over the Black Hills. With 268 U.S. forces killed, the battle was memorialized in history books, in part because it provided justification for additional U.S. forces to engage in combat. Less than a year later, the land was annexed by the United States and reservations were established for the Native Americans.

As Robert explained the conflict to his son, he was genuinely moved looking upon a field of so much history. He explains in detail the changing colors of the skies, how the grass under his fingers was sharp, almost cutting like razor blades. "I felt almost like I could see the remnants of the gunpowder from that battle all those many years ago," he recounts poetically. "I thought about the final moments of the people who lost their lives there, all of those people with their thick and empty heads. And I thought about the people with the same empty-mindedness, protected by Plexiglas and armor, in Standing Rock. I thought about how the same empty-mindedness could last for so long. And I was sad that we have been in conflict with these peoples for so long."

When they finally arrived at Standing Rock, Robert was energized. Staying in the third teepee from the entrance of the warrior camp, the family knew all of the comings and goings. They were mesmerized when the Navajo riders came running into camp atop their frothy horses. People arrived from all over the country to make a stand; over 500 members of the clergy joined an interfaith ceremony to bring attention to the issue. "I was constantly in prayer," Robert remembers, thinking of the armed police dressed in riot gear. "We were on high alert. We were doing normal things like preparing food, chopping wood, and organizing camp security. But we knew that anything could happen at any second." Still, looking at police with their "goofy" black hats and boots, Robert almost thought that they looked like little bugs rather than like a substantial threat.

It was the second day at Standing Rock when Robert claims that a reporter who had been chasing after him finally got in touch—a difficult task considering that Standing Rock didn't have regular phone service. He remembers exactly what he was looking at when he was giving the interview. "There were colors all around me. To the top of the sun, there was white; to the bottom of the sun, there was aqua," he comments. "There were people all around and the sounds of the military and the helicopters were causing so much disruption to the harmony. People couldn't sleep because of all of the noise." To Robert, it felt like the world was diseased and when the reporter asked if he was going to vote for Hillary Clinton, he responded, "No, no, no, no; she's not getting my vote."

According to Robert, he was thinking about what was right and wrong. He had spent the last several months with his family. This time was inspiring him to think about what his legacy would be once he passed on. "I try to be a holy man," Robert admits. "I pass down teachings to my children and they pass them down to my grandchildren. I began to think about what my legacy would be like if I voted for Hillary." Robert was worried about what her presidency would look like; how things could go haywire. He imagined how his children, grandchildren, and great-grandchildren would rationalize his legacy. "I am against everything that Hillary was for, so would they think to themselves that I was a hypocrite, for saying one thing and doing another?"

The only problem is that Robert had signed a pledge earlier saying that he would vote for Clinton. Robert is a man of concepts and big ideas; dates and details seem to be evasive in our conversations. But Robert mentioned that on August 9th he had received an email asking the Washington electors to sign a pledge promising that they would vote for Clinton. Robert had an unusual feeling about this pledge. "We Indians understand the limitations of a piece of paper," he now comments. "So, I saw this pledge and I thought about all of the treaties that were signed and not honored or that actively hurt us." Robert thought that he would go ahead and sign his name: "it is nothing but a piece of paper," he reasoned.

Robert didn't have a second thought about his talk with the reporter, until he and his family decided to stop into the Prairie Knights Casino so that Sonny Boy could warm up a bit. Robert's phone had run out of battery, so he took the opportunity to charge up. Once he turned it back on, he knew something was off: it just kept pinging with one notification and missed call after another. It was clear that a lot of people were trying to get hold of him. Robert opened up one of the messages and saw a strong curse word, which he said that he was never going to repeat. Once he read one of these messages, he found himself reading one angry message after another; people he claims were infuriated after his interview had gained traction in the middle of the day. "Each message was such a message of hate," Robert remembers. "My feelings were hurt so bad. I was confused: why would people who don't even know me say these things to me? I try to be a holy man; this was the last thing that I expected."

When Elizabeth found out that Robert was dealing with this, she tried to pry the phone away from her husband, saying that he was clearly on some list and that he just needed to let everyone calm down. However, Robert's mother (whom he describes as a "mother bear") had the final say: She asked him if he had succeeded in sharing his vision with Faith. When he said that he had, she said that he needed to come home—his name was everywhere, even on the Rachel Maddow show that she liked to watch. "You have to come here and take care of your business," she told Robert, "There are enough people out there in Standing Rock." As Robert began to think about the last couple of days, he felt strongly that his mission was complete. After a short discussion, Robert and Elizabeth decided it was time to head back home. They were worried about whether tensions between the protestors and law enforcement might escalate and what sort of effect that might have on their preteen son, who was starting to cling to Robert when he went out for protests.

Just as suddenly as they had dropped everything to drive to Standing Rock, they picked up everything to head back to Tacoma. Elizabeth drove, as Robert started responding to messages. He formulated responses to all of the hate: "Thank you for expressing your concerns with me. What you say matters. I love you." But after Robert would press send, he was surprised by his recipients' reactions. "They didn't read it out of love; they read it as some sort of provocation and they would say awful and vile things in response," Robert recalls. "By then, I had decided that they themselves were confused; they were hurting and didn't have the right way to express themselves." Robert thought that they had not been taught how to take care of their emotional needs in ways that were taught to indigenous people at young ages—by singing their song.

Elizabeth thought that Robert was still being foolish by engaging with internet trolls: "What did you expect would happen after that interview?" she asked Robert. But Robert decided that he was going to respond regardless, with unconditional love, and that he was not going to have the insults penetrate his psyche. "By the fifth back-and-forth with these people, they quit saying bad things. I know that I was making breakthroughs." Robert was feeling compassion for many hurt people, and feeling the need to pray for them. As they neared their home, Robert turned to Elizabeth and told her that he was feeling inspired by the reiteration of the truth that love can conquer all.

Getting home late at night, Robert was feeling optimistic. He began to think about doing something particularly special for Elizabeth—he was going to get some tickets for the upcoming Seattle Seahawks game for Monday Night football. When they arrived home, Elizabeth, who had driven most of the way, started getting ready for bed, and Robert's mother came down to start getting Sonny Boy ready for bed.

Robert started grabbing the luggage from the car and bringing pieces inside one after another, when suddenly his plans for Monday Night football dissipated. All of a sudden, he saw an SUV with its bright lights on facing his house diagonally. He had never seen anything quite like it, and his heart immediately ran cold. Doubts started flooding into his head. He began to think that he had probably done the one thing that could have pissed off the most politically powerful couple in the country. "I had heard these backroom whispers of stuff like superdelegates getting killed. And I know that things like this can be untraceable."

Robert convinced himself that he might just be making things up in his head, so he decided to go out and get another load of things to bring back inside. While outside, he saw that the car had come even closer and had turned off its lights. He rushed back inside with fear pulsating through his veins, trying to make things look normal. He turned off all the lights, peeked out through the window blinds, looking at the slow movement of the car, and made sure everything was locked.

Robert claims that he had no idea what to do. He texted a buddy who he knew had a gun saying that he was feeling unsafe. He then suddenly remembered that he had the contact of someone from Jill Stein's team from Standing Rock, who had told him to call if the family encountered anything out of the ordinary. They picked up almost immediately and asked him if he was safe. When Robert said that a car had followed them home, he was shocked by how quickly they jumped into action. "Immediately, they started talking about getting me to a safe house. They told me to start preparing the family for extraction; that they were going to get us out of there." Robert admits that he wasn't comprehending what they were asking. "They were asking me questions that I had never thought of: Did I want to separate the family or not? Did I want to hide somewhere local or outside of the area? They told me to grab all of our cell phones and wrap them with tin foil." Robert was getting more and more scared; he knew that everyone who knew him thought they were still at Standing Rock. In his mind, his family could go missing without a trace.

Robert heard a crack; the sound of someone pushing in the door. At that one moment, he was sure that his life was over. When he looked up, he didn't see an assassin, however. He saw his old buddy, who is a purple heart veteran. And his buddy didn't come alone; he came with a group of friends. They were carrying such heavy firepower that Robert claims that he hadn't seen anything like it before. He was shocked. On the phone, he heard the voice of Jill Stein's team, who were worried by all of the commotion. "I had never prayed with Stein's people; I didn't really know them. I had this strong feeling that whatever happened next, it needed to be with people I had prayed with."

Robert went upstairs and told his family of the sudden turn of events. They were clearly petrified. Once again, they were leaving the house in darkness. His buddy turned out to have a network of safe houses; so Robert decided to split up the family. His mother went to one; the immediate family went to another. Sonny Boy wasn't allowed to go to school. "We stayed there up until election night," Robert comments. "I figured once it was clear that Hillary wasn't going to win the election anyway, it was probably safe for us to go back home."

Art Sisneros
Part 2

A rt Sisneros had no intention of running for an elector at the Texas Republican State Convention in May 2016. In fact, he had never run for any political position in his entire life. Even if he did, he was unsure if he could actually win it. He had been a late bloomer to politics and had only been brought into the fold through Texas Congressman Ron Paul's presidential bids in 2008 and 2012. Ron Paul himself was a bit of an outsider in the Republican Party. In fact, he left the Republicans in 1987, running for President on the Libertarian Party ticket in 1988, before coming back to the Republicans in 1996.

The day before the election to determine the electors, Art remembers that he was approached by another man whom he vaguely knew from Ron Paul's Liberty Movement. He suggested that Art should run as an elector. "He said that if we got a lot of electors in Texas, we could make the election interesting," Art recalls. "I still am not one hundred percent sure what he meant by that comment." Regardless, Art found himself Googling what the Electoral College was the night before, gleaning a basic understanding of it, and deciding that he would give it a shot.

In hindsight, Art says that he really had no idea what he was signing up for when he began campaigning for elector the next morning. It was the last day of the Texas State Convention and he needed to convince the 300 delegates at the 36th Congress District's breakout session that he would be a good elector for them. Relatively new to the party, Art saw a lot of new faces he had never met before, as well as a lot of faces that just showed up to big events like the convention. However, when Art began his campaign for elector, he realized that he knew quite a large number of people, who he hoped could vouch for him when push came to shove. He noted that his emphasis on local political engagement gave him an additional advantage in the 36th District because he knew a broad spectrum of people from all over their geographically spread-out and largely rural district (one of only two districts in Texas that has never been represented by a Democrat.)

Art forgets how many people were running—but he thinks it was either six or seven. Although Art didn't have much experience in politics, he did have a lot of experience giving talks at church and he felt that his charisma gave him an edge over the other candidates. Another thing which distinguished him was his age: most of the other candidates were older men. They were die-hard Republicans who always showed up and had already checked a number of honorary titles off their list. Art believes that most of them were trying to be electors as a last hurrah of sorts before winding down their political involvement.

Interestingly, Art doesn't remember a traditional Republican establishment candidate in his race. "In Texas, our big thing is becoming a delegate to the Republican National Convention," he comments. "It is a real buddy club and there is no way that a normal person can get in there. You have to be in line to get that position." By contrast, the Electoral College vote seemed almost like an afterthought. "We spent the whole week hashing out platform issues. Choosing an elector felt like the last thing we had to do before going home."

In his speech to become an elector, Art talked mostly about his Christian faith. He doesn't remember the details, but he remembers the basic gist, commenting that he tried to represent who he is as a person, and that he hasn't changed very much since then. "I talked about liberty and the dangers of trusting in the state," he recalls. Also, after having done a bit of searching around on the internet the night before, Art decided to share his initial views on the Electoral College system itself. "I mentioned American history and how there was nothing that exemplified the difference between a republic and a democracy more than the Electoral College."

When Art was selected as the elector, he was a bit shocked. He later sought out the acquaintance in the Liberty Movement who had suggested that he run in the first place. It was then that he discovered that the man's plans were dashed when Art was the only one who managed to become an elector. They went their separate ways and Art didn't talk to him again.

"When this happened, I didn't have this feeling of grand honor. I was more curious than anything else. I thought that there might be more to it than I actually knew," Art says. "For sure, I didn't think that it was some meaningless thing, because I had heard about the Electoral College before. I knew it was big. But I didn't know how or why." Indeed, throughout our conversation, Art often returns to his overall lack of knowledge about the Electoral College, as well as that of the people who elected him into office. He comments that he often wonders why the choosing of electors wasn't treated as a bigger deal at the State Convention.

Describing himself as a "radical," Art comments that once he decides to do something, he is all-in. In this case, Art decided that he was going to learn everything that he could about the Electoral College to satisfy his curiosity about what it actually was, beginning an intensive period of research. The more he researched, the happier he became that he had decided to homeschool his children. He was shocked how such an important component of electing the President was not studied extensively in school, commenting, "Subjects are brought into children's minds, ripped out of history and context. They are pieces of information that are forgotten because they have nothing to stick to. Looking into the Electoral College confirmed that homeschooling was definitely the best option for our kids."

As Art describes his research to me, it comes across like a bottomless pit (a sentiment which I understand all too well due to my own research on the Electoral College.) The deeper he dug into the Electoral College and why it was originally started, the deeper he felt he needed to dig to find the answer. Fascinated by what he was learning, Art describes many a night reading late until 1 A.M. or 2 A.M. about the Electoral College, the early years of the American Republic, and the Founding Fathers.

He started his reading with Alexander Hamilton and The Federalist Papers. He then jumped to the relatively lesser-known Anti-Federalist Papers, a collection of rebuttal works that was not even compiled into a book until 1965. After reading the original sources, Art began to look for scholars with a similar worldview to his own to provide perspective into his duty as an elector. Although he devoured dozens of books, the one that most influenced his thoughts on the Electoral College was *The Evolution and Destruction of the Original Electoral College*, written by self-proclaimed freedom coaches Gary and Carolyn Alder. Focusing on the differences between a republic and a democracy, the husband-wife author team delved into the Founders' intent for the Electoral College before the creation of political parties and the subsequent ratification of the Twelfth Amendment.

However, that wasn't deep enough for Art, who really wanted to get into the mindset of the Founding Fathers when they created the Electoral College. Two other books that influenced his thoughts were *Roger Sherman and the Creation of the American Republic* by Mark David Hall and *The Roots of the American Republic* by Reverend E.C. Wines. Through these readings, he came to the belief that while the Founding Fathers may not have shared all of his own personal beliefs and faith, they still lived within a system with a certain set of values. "I got an understanding of how Christian ideas impacted what the Founders' understanding of what republicanism was—how the concept of republicanism was developed in the church and the family and later applied to the state," Art summarizes as his take-aways. It was this definition of a republic that he took to heart as he considered his role and responsibility as an elector.

In Art's mind, he delineated his Electoral College vote from his personal vote. He had decided early on that he could not justify voting Trump for President. In the 2016 primary, he supported Kentucky Senator Rand Paul, albeit, a bit unenthusiastically. He believed that there was a vast difference between Rand Paul and his father Ron, the political figure who had inspired Art to join politics in the first place. The difference was so pronounced that Art was willing to vote for Rand, but unwilling to donate any time or money. When it came to Trump, Art comments that from a political perspective, "he was very much unknown in regard to his consistency on issues. There was no track record to base him on, except for him saying stuff on Twitter." However, he felt that Trump was a man who was not Biblically qualified to be President.

Leading up to the November election, Art had a feeling that Trump was going to win. Regardless, he knew that Trump was going to win Texas and that he would be called on to be an elector. As he was grappling with this role, Art began to write down his ideas. Even though he didn't have an advanced education, he found that the research process came quite naturally to him and he strived to write logically and clearly, like the books he enjoyed reading. "I was trying to piece together what made sense according to my conscience and my beliefs. That is how my blog posts came about. I was just making sense of the things I was reading." On November 7, the day before the election, he posted "Biblical Voting in the Age of Trump" on his Blessed Path blog page. With a hunch that Trump was going to win, he wanted to go ahead and get his ideas out there in the open.

In an over 3,000-word treatise, Art delves deeply into Biblical scripture to discuss his reasons for not voting for Donald Trump for President. Unlike many of his contemporaries, who delved into Trump's specific actions, Art focused on Biblical examples, prefacing them by stating that Trump had done things "too depraved to be repeated" on his blog. Reading his blog post, it is obvious that his audience is clearly not the general public, but likely comprised of people in his religious community who were conflicted about having Trump as the Republican nominee.

Noting the argument that many Biblical leaders fell short of God's standards, including the Hebrew kings Saul, David, and Solomon, and that God was still able to work through them, Art supports his claim by quoting scriptures from 1 Samuel and 2 Chronicles. He notes that, "each of these men sinned greatly against the Lord during their administration, but that doesn't mean they weren't qualified at the time they were chosen. The qualifications of being godly men who fear the Lord and are able to rule justly does not require perfection."

At the end of his post, he tries to counter an argument that many Republicans may have faced during this time—that Donald Trump was the lesser of two evils and that Republicans should subsequently vote for Trump to stop Clinton from winning. However, Art comments:

> *I can understand this position for there is no doubt that Hillary Clinton would be an evil President, but would she really be more evil than Trump in policy? Rather than going to the talking points of the political parties and inside operatives, let's look at the biggest issues that actually matter. If we look at where they stand on the monetary policy of the Federal Reserve, murdering of unborn children, undeclared wars, the complete disregard for private property, or our national debt, the only difference between the two is in style and rhetoric. Where it matters most, they will both pursue the same wicked policies. Even if I am wrong about their policies, and one is slightly better than the other, it still would not make it an ethically righteous decision to suddenly throw off the qualifications in hope of possibly having a slightly less evil government.*

While it might have seemed to outsiders that Art was grappling with whether to vote for Trump, Art stipulates that he had made up his mind about that a long time before. He didn't vote for Trump in the primaries, nor would he in the general election. What Art was grappling with was whether he should vote for Trump in his role as an elector. "What I was wrestling with was the challenge that, as an elector, I was going to be casting my vote on behalf of other people," he comments. At the same time, as Art notes on his friends' The Liberty Line podcast on November 27, 2016, he was trying to consider what was truly in the best interest of his district. He said, "I cannot vote for Trump because I do not think it is in the best interest of my district to rebel against God's word . . . or else we should expect the judgement of God."

He thought long and hard about the implications of his article before posting it. But he was not really considering about his decision's long-term effects on the Electoral College. He was mostly thinking that going public with his struggle as a Christian might have an impact on others also struggling with voting for Trump. "I thought it would be good for people to see the example of someone accepting the consequence of standing up for their convictions, whatever the consequences were. I think that few people discuss the ethics of their faith in a public way. This wasn't just about the Electoral College; it was about a Christian being consistent." For Art, this was also another opportunity to teach his children, by being an example of "someone who was full of grace in the midst of struggle."

What Art was not expecting was for the election to blow up, for the Hamilton Electors to start trying to woo Republican electors, and for electors to take on a public image. Everything was about to go "insane," and Art would soon find himself in the middle of firing squads from the left, right, and middle of the political spectrum for his blog post.

Micheal Baca
Part 2

It was the night of the election and Micheal Baca was in downtown Denver watching the election results coming in. "The closer it got to the election, I got more and more of a sense that Trump might actually be able to win this thing," Micheal remembers of that night. The thought of Trump winning scared him immensely; he was convinced that Trump was a danger to American democracy. But Micheal kept most of these doubts to himself. He had made a large new circle of friends, all in progressive politics, who now surrounded him at what he describes as a "pretty fancy election party," through his tenure as an alternate delegate to the Democratic National Convention in Philadelphia a few months prior. "In my political community, there was an echo chamber of support for Hillary, even though I kind of knew that this point of view was extremely limited," he comments.

Micheal's friends became increasingly emotional, as one key state after another was called for Trump and Hillary's loss seemed more and more imminent. The celebratory alcohol quickly became a way to rid themselves of despair and Micheal remembers that people started getting tipsy. One of his friends came up to him and said, "I was a national delegate; but I can't do anything now. But you, you can do something: you are an elector." This comment, from a person Micheal had grown to respect deeply, stirred a sentiment deep inside of him: he had the power to try to make things right.

Prior to the election, Micheal had been approached by Bret Chiafalo, an elector out of Washington state. Micheal claims that Bret was interested in using the election as a mechanism to promote Electoral College reform. The plan was nebulous at best, as Bret was sure that Clinton was going to win and wasn't sure what to do after that. As Micheal sat watching the vote come in, he began to think that maybe Bret's idea could be expanded to keep Trump out of office. He remembers, "I kept thinking to myself that there are still 40-odd days to stop a demagogue from taking office because the real vote didn't actually happen yet." Too upset to get a good night's rest, he stayed up texting ideas back and forth with his friends. By 8:30 A.M., he had reached out to Bret, saying that he wanted to work with him to come up with a plan.

He remembers being influenced by an exit poll that said only something like 25% of Republicans voted for Trump because he was backed by the GOP, not because they supported his candidacy or liked who he was as a person. He wondered whether if Democratic electors offered to vote for a moderate Republican candidate, Republican electors might jump on the chance to vote for a candidate they truly believed in. "My thought process was basically this," explains Micheal. "If I voted for Hillary, Trump would definitely win regardless. But what if I decided to do something different? Maybe I could change the minds of 37 Republican electors, and that would keep Trump from getting the necessary majority to win. When I looked at it like that, there was really only one choice at the end of the day."

Micheal's loyalty to the Democratic Party was doubtlessly impacted by his tenure at the DNC. Even though he tries to focus our conversations solely on the Electoral College, memories from the DNC pour over. "Overall, I enjoyed the convention. It all happened too quickly, but it was really amazing to be there and experience it firsthand," he remembers. However, it was also at the DNC that Micheal engaged in his first act of civil disobedience, in protest against Bernie Sanders's treatment.

Describing it as akin to "living through a commercial," Micheal was surprised by how all of the products and merchandise seemed to only focus on Clinton, even when Sanders still had a shot in his eyes (as well as in the eyes of many, some of whom were saying things along the lines of "a vote for Clinton means that Trump will win.") The rifts between the Sanders and the Clinton camps were tense in the state elections and caucuses, and continued to be intense at the DNC.

In the convention hall, Micheal and his fellow progressive Colorado friends were wearing neon yellow shirts to try to get the attention of the media, shouting in unison, "Enough is enough." When the lights were turned off in their section, Micheal proudly notes that they stood out even more than before, with their neon shirts glowing in the dark. "I would have preferred us just sitting down until they forcibly removed us in front of all of the cameras rolling. That would have gotten a lot of attention," Micheal remembers, "Instead, we ended up doing this sit-in at the media tent. I wasn't interviewed, but I was there. It was my first time ever doing something like that, something like civil disobedience. And I liked it."

When he returned to Colorado after the Convention, the idea struck Micheal: just because he was an elector, he no longer felt compelled to vote for Clinton just for the sake of voting for Clinton. He needed to vote for himself and who he believed to be the right choice for President. Around the same time he started talking with Bret, he began to do his own research on the Electoral College, beginning with Alexander Hamilton's Federalist Paper No. 68. "The more I learned about the Electoral College, the more I began to feel moved by the responsibility that it entailed," Micheal comments. "I realized that by voting for who I believed to be the right candidate, I was actually being faithful to the Constitution." Disagreeing with the term "faithless electors," he also pored over Article 2 of the Constitution, the Twelfth Amendment, and Cornell Law Notes to back up this new interpretation of his role and rights as an elector.

"I think because I was anticipating Trump's win, I was ready to jump on it and start doing something," Micheal says. The day after the general election, he remembers that he spent about 17 hours on the phone with Bret Chiafalo to come up with a plan. "I was such a political novice. I didn't really have a clue on what I needed to do," Micheal remembers, mentioning that he began writing all of the contacts that he met through the DNC with his plan. Most were not receptive, saying that even if enough Republicans defected to make sure that Trump didn't get the 270 votes necessary for a majority, the House of Representatives would probably vote in favor of Trump anyway, just to ensure social stability.

Their feedback (or lack thereof) didn't impact Micheal at all. He tried to contact Ohio Governor and Republican moderate John Kasich several times to see if he might be on board with the plan. Figuring that his messages probably "ended up getting lost on some desk in the Governor's mansion," Micheal notes that, "I wouldn't have done this if anyone else had won the presidency. I wouldn't even have done this for Ted Cruz. I just think that Donald Trump was different from all of the rest."

Calling themselves the "moral electors," meaning that they were planning on voting their moral conscience during the Electoral College vote rather than according to their states' popular votes, Micheal and Bret started to get attention. "Everything changed for us with our first CNN piece," Micheal remembers. "The emails and the phone calls just started pouring in. People with political know-how and professionals were wanting to help us."

One of the people who had jumped on board early was a mysterious Mr. D, who Micheal flat-out claims, "if you are going to have a villain in this story, I think that he might be the one." Mr. D was a young man from Texas, who called himself a "reformed Republican" and offered to open up his vast network of Republican resources and donors, who presumably wanted to keep Trump out of office. Micheal now doubts his credibility, thinking that Mr. D even could have been a mole from the Republican Party to thwart his plan. Even now, he says that Mr. D continues to have a very elusive online presence. At the time, however, Mr. D's claims that he worked as a political appointee in the George W. Bush administration, backed up with photos of him with the President and Vice President Dick Cheney, made him seem to be one of the perfect individuals to make the "moral electors" into a truly bipartisan effort.

One of Mr. D's first suggestions was to rename the movement, making the case that the name "Hamilton Electors" might gain more traction than the "moral electors," particularly among conservatives who revered the Constitution. "It makes sense," Micheal concedes. "Not only is Hamilton a Founding Father, but if you call yourself a 'moral elector' and claimed to be on the high ground, a lot of conservatives might immediately reject it."

The moniker seemed to stick: they incorporated the Hamilton Electors as a 527 organization in the state of Nevada (a tax-exempt organization, which most political organizations, including committees, parties, and PACs register as) on November 29, 2016. In many ways, Mr. D seemed like a lifesaver at the time, as Micheal was busy working to make ends meet and Bret worked nights and slept during the days.

With Micheal, Bret, and the pro-bono Mr. D in three different states, it would come as no surprise that the fledgling Hamilton Electors faced a number of miscommunications, which Micheal claims led to a great deal of drama. Although he was designated as the President of the Hamilton Electors, Micheal became very frustrated, feeling as if he was left out of the making of key decisions. "From the beginning, I had the same strategy. All I wanted to do was talk to the biggest fish I could find and try to convince them of our way of thinking," Micheal asserts. "I didn't think that there was going to be enough time to build something grassroots, something that could change hearts and minds." He was shocked when real money started pouring in from outside donors and the Hamilton Electors used the money to organize events like candlelight vigils in front of State Houses around the country (which he claims was masterminded by Mr. D).

"If I had been involved in that decision-making process, I would have vetoed it for sure," Micheal says, who claims that he was out of the loop. "I think they were supposed to be heart-warming somehow; inspiring and convincing people to do the right thing through happiness. But at the end of the day, were they the most effective?" Realizing that his influence over the Hamilton Electors was ultimately limited, he began to formulate bold new plans to keep Trump out of office, which he would soon pitch to anyone who would listen.

Bret Chiafalo
Part 2

"The first few days of the Hamilton Electors were just us spinning our wheels; trying desperately to get our message heard above all of the noise," Bret comments. Remembering the country as in a state of utter meltdown after Donald Trump won the presidential election, Bret thought it would take nothing short of a miracle to get the organization to the next level. Not that they had much of an organization anyway—all they really had was an idea and a Facebook page. Bret didn't have a lot of disposable income, but started boosting posts with the hopes that they would be able to get in front of the right people.

Bret had been taken by surprise: he was not expecting Donald Trump to win. In fact, when Trump got the Republican Party nomination that summer, Bret was excited. "In hindsight, this clearly was not the right interpretation of what was happening, but I thought that Trump getting the nomination was the best thing that could possibly happen for the Democrats. I thought that the Republicans had flushed their chance of winning down the tubes," Bret stipulates. Although Bret doesn't say this directly, his thoughts may have been influenced by the few conservatives in his social circle: namely, his parents.

Fans of Ronald Reagan, Bret's parents were so disappointed in Trump's win that they decided that they would cast their votes for the Democrats instead. "Sure, they might have thought that they were voting for Clinton because her name was the one on the ballot, but they were really just voting for me as an elector to vote for her on their behalf," Bret facetiously adds, before noting that his parents were "utterly disgusted" by Trump and the anti-intellectualism that he brought to his campaign.

Although he admits that some Bernie supporters were pulled over to the Trump side after the Democratic National Convention "just because they didn't want to see the same-old same-old in office," Bret was sure that Clinton was going to win. He didn't feel the need to volunteer for her campaign and decided to spend his free time researching the Electoral College instead. He was still struggling with what it meant to be an elector who campaigned on the premise of being against the Electoral College.

Working the night shifts at the X-Box Command Center, Bret found himself with some time to kill, and estimated that he probably spent about 20 hours a week researching the Electoral College throughout the summer. "I discovered very fast that most people who are considered to be experts on the Electoral College have absolutely no clue what they are talking about," he asserts, "So I quit looking for other people's interpretations of what the Electoral College was and tried to go straight to the primary sources."

Besides reading Senate debates, court documents, and letters from the Founding Fathers, he also started researching how other states chose their electors. He was horrified to learn that the New York Democrats had an executive committee to choose their electors ("that is how Bill Clinton became an elector"), as well as the California system. "Since California Democratic electors are appointed directly by House Members, Nancy Pelosi chose her own daughter, Christine!" he exclaims. In the instances when he couldn't find information about how the state parties chose their electors online, he took it to the next level: getting on the phone or e-mailing state parties with his questions.

When deciding what to do about his own personal vote, Bret discovered that the state of Washington had some of the strictest laws against faithless electors, stemming from Republican elector Mike Padden's faithless vote in 1976. Now a state senator representing part of Washington's Spokane County, in 1976 Mike was a thirty-year-old whippersnapper who denied Republican Gerald Ford his Electoral College vote. He opted to give it to then-California governor Ronald Reagan instead. Reporter David Ammons recalls Padden's faithless vote at the Washington State House as chaotic: "there were a lot of people [with] eyebrows raised and wondering what to do, but there was no prescription against it, other than he didn't do what he was supposed to do by everybody's expectation." In response, the Washington legislature required all electors, regardless of party, to sign pledges and pay $1,000 if they defected (the equivalent of $4,500 in today's currency.)

Padden blasted the decision as unconstitutional. Although Bret certainly agreed with Padden's assessment, the more he researched, the more he realized that pledges were complicated: some state laws required them, some didn't, and sometimes parties required their own pledges, regardless of state law. Most of Bret's understanding of the matter was ultimately influenced by the *Ray v. Blair* court case that was argued at the Supreme Court in 1952. Essentially, an Alabama Democrat elector refused to sign a pledge that Alabama's Democratic Party had requested him to sign. The Court ruled that political parties could indeed ask the electors to sign a pledge, but noted that any efforts that parties made to enforce the pledge were likely to be unconstitutional.

"Even though it is clear that the Constitution beats out any pledge, I consider myself a man of ethics and honor," Bret comments. Even though he had considered the possibility of voting for Sanders in the Electoral College as a way to test the Washington state law, when faced with the pledge, Bret was torn. "When I read it, I really didn't think that I could break a pledge like that. When I signed it, I didn't take it lightly. I thought that Clinton was going to win the election and I had every intention of voting for her for President at that time."

Meanwhile, Bret says that he was going a bit stir-crazy with all of the knowledge he was acquiring about the Electoral College and not having anyone to share it with. "It's not like you can go outside and talk with your neighbor about the Electoral College," he says. "They have no clue and really no interest in learning about it." Normally, when Bret really got into a subject, he would try to reach out to a like-minded community by joining some internet chat rooms or Facebook groups to talk over strategies and ideas. By contrast, the self-proclaimed extrovert found himself with no outlet to discuss the Electoral College. Then he came up with a fantastic idea: he would reach out to the other eleven Democratic electors in Washington to discuss the Electoral College with them. That is how he ended up connecting with future Hamilton Electors Levi Guerra and Esther "Little Dove" John.

Normally, he began a conversation by talking about how much he disagreed with the Electoral College in principle. He was upset that out of the entire state, their twelve votes were the only ones that mattered. He admits that a lot of their conversations were just about theory, with him sometimes going on wild tangents about what might happen if they all collectively decided to vote for Bernie Sanders instead. Other times, he would discuss how people needed to take a stand, just so that the Supreme Court could determine whether or not the Electoral College was just a rubber stamp.

In my conversation with Bret, he stresses that he didn't have any plans to do anything out of others' expectations. These were just hypotheticals that he was throwing out there to anyone who would listen. When he ran out of Washington electors to talk to, he reached out to the Democratic electors in Colorado and Alaska, because he had learned through his research that they were chosen in a similar method as the Washington electors. Sometimes, he would read out the primary sources that he had been collecting. One of his favorites was Alexander Hamilton's "The Mode of Electing the President." Written under the pen name Publius, the 1,500-word essay made up Number 68 of The Federalist Papers, and suggested that the Electoral College:

> ... be made by men most capable of analyzing the qualities adapted to the station, and acting under circumstances favorable to deliberation, and to a judicious combination of all the reasons and inducements which were proper to govern their choice. A small number of persons, selected by their fellow-citizens from the general mass, will be most likely to possess the information and discernment requisite to such complicated investigations.

On the day of the November election, Bret woke up at his normal 3 P.M. to start getting ready for his night shift. The polls were already starting to close on the East Coast and Bret could see that it was not going to be the clean sweep for Clinton that many thought it might be. As he drove to work, things were looking bad. Once his shift started, things started to look worse and worse. "It was brutal and it was a complete shock to me," Bret comments. "It came out of nowhere." Sometime during that shift, Bret got a call from a distraught elector whom he had reached out to earlier, Colorado elector Micheal Baca, to discuss the election and throw around more hypotheticals. Was it possible that they could do something as electors to stop Trump from taking office? Bret and Micheal agreed that Trump was exactly the type of candidate that Hamilton warned against in Federalist Number 68:

> *The process of [the Electoral College] affords a moral certainty, that the office of President will never fall to the lot of any man who is not in an eminent degree endowed with the requisite qualifications.*

For the first few minutes, he remembers that they were still trying to think up ideas that would ensure that Clinton would get the presidency. "But no matter how we discussed it, the numbers just didn't work," Bret remembers. "At that point, it became very obvious. Once we got rid of the possibility of electing Hillary, we landed on the idea of getting enough electors to vote for another Republican to throw the election to the House of Representatives." Once they decided upon this idea of getting 37 Republicans to defect so that the provisions of the Twelfth Amendment could kick in, they had no idea how to start acting on that idea to make it a reality. Bret asked a Sanders activist he knew in Washington state, Shawn Comfort, to help them gain some traction locally. Together, the three of them spent the next three days desperately trying to get the message out through their "moral electors" Facebook page.

"There was so much noise on the internet. There were websites and petitions and groups starting letter-writing campaigns to all of the

Republican electors to convince them to vote for Hillary," Bret remembers of those early chaotic days. He claims that from Day One, he knew what they were trying to do was a Hail Mary and had less than a 1% chance of working; but he felt that even that 1% chance was worth it to stop what he describes as a "sexual-assaulting demagogue" from taking the office of the President.

But there were initial challenges. The three of them were unlikely founders of a major political movement. Bret was working nights, and Micheal and Shawn were both in their early twenties. All of them were Sanders supporters and "Bernie people didn't have any establishment connections." In his assessment, none of them had the professional ability to take this to the next level, let alone do so in the mere 40 days before the December 19 vote. He was incredibly relieved when a political operative named Mr. D reached out to them, willing to open up his network of contacts. "If we didn't bring him on, I am not sure if we would have gotten ourselves heard over all of that noise," Bret admits. "To grow, we had to bring in people with logistical skills that we didn't have. Basically, the only thing I offered to the team was that I was halfway decent in front of the media and I had been researching the Electoral College like a MOFO for months. I had no organizational skills whatsoever."

Mr. D kept encouraging them to simplify their message, eventually suggesting that they change the name to the Hamilton Electors to better reach out to conservatives. "By the end, the message was so simplified that we would just mention Federalist 68 in an interview and say that we were standing up for what the Founding Fathers wanted," Bret remembers.

When they got an interview on Fox News with famed conservative political commentator Tucker Carlson, Bret realized that the Hamilton Electors had a shot at making a difference. In his opinion, it was the ultimate place to get their message out to people who didn't share their opinions and their views. Bret saw a substantial number of new threats against his life after the interview, about which he comments, "I thought about the phrase: 'You have enemies? Good. That means you've stood up for something, sometime in your life.' I reminded myself that what I was standing up for was actually a constitutional responsibility."

When asked if he was scared by the threats, he answers in the affirmative. "I tried to contact the local sheriffs," he laughs, "But they kind of just thought I was a crazy man. They really had no understanding of what the Electoral College was or how my life might be endangered as an elector." He stipulates that there was no time to contact the FBI, describing the 40 days before the Electoral College vote as a complete blur. He was working 40 hours a week and dedicating another 60 hours a week to the Hamilton Electors. Even with the 60 hours he was spending on the nascent movement, he never felt like there was enough time to do everything that needed to be done. He was skipping meals, forcing himself to eat whenever he remembered. Sleep often proved elusive.

Bret still loved talking to the electors, but realized that it was one task that he needed to offload to the ever-growing team under Mr. D. Bret estimates that he talked with about 50 Republican electors and an additional 10–20 Democratic electors on behalf of the Hamilton Electors. "Some made it clear that they had no interest in what I was talking about," he recalls. "Others said that they also had concerns about Trump, but that they were afraid that the Hamilton Electors was a trick to get Clinton elected." Collectively, it was decided that as an elector himself, Bret needed to be up in front of the cameras, rather behind a phone trying to contact other electors. Armed with an Excel spreadsheet and a script that Bret had supervised, there were Hamilton Electors volunteers to help out with that task.

Bret did enjoy going on the media, commenting that his favorite interview was with the Swiss Public Radio. "I just remember hearing the sound of my voice and then my voice being dubbed over by this absolutely gorgeous and sexy French accent," he laughs. "I thought it was just so funny. I think that the Hamilton Electors just sounded so much better coming out of his mouth."

From a PR perspective, Bret realized that the movement was limited if it was just him and Micheal, two Democratic white male electors. His worries ebbed when Washington Democratic elector Levi Guerra came out publicly in support as a Hamilton Elector, along with Texas Republican elector Chris Suprun (who with the Hamilton Electors' help also managed to get his scathing op-ed "Why I Will Not Cast My Electoral Vote for Donald Trump" published by the *New York Times*). As Bret began to think about the future, he wondered if maybe their crazy idea wasn't a Hail Mary after all.

The Scholar
Part 1

"There are a lot of gaps when it comes to the Electoral College because most academics don't think it is really that important at the end of the day. After all, it only comes around once every four years. In graduate school, I don't remember it being mentioned at all," Robert Alexander comments. As the Director of the Institute for Civics and Public Policy at Ohio Northern University in Ada, Ohio, Rob is one of the only academics in the country dedicated to studying the mechanism that selects the President of the United States.

It didn't start out that way, though. "My research was originally interest groups, which I have dropped entirely," Rob laughs. "I never would have dreamed that before. But, this change in my research was kind of a happy surprise."

Rob's awareness of the Electoral College was sparked by one of his professors at the University of Tennessee in Knoxville, where he was attending graduate school. As a first-generation college student, Rob had found himself in academia almost by accident and was very much influenced by the suggestions of his professors. Originally, he had wanted to attend law school, when one of his undergraduate professors at Ohio Northern University saw him tutor another student in political science and commented that he would make a good professor. Rob remembers his teacher mentioning that they actually paid for people to attend school and become professors. With his interest piqued, Rob changed his career path and jumped headfirst into academia, even though he didn't understand exactly what it entailed.

When his graduate school professor approached Rob and suggested that they do some research into the electors of the Electoral College together, Rob agreed. "He thought it might make a good footnote in American government textbooks," Rob remembers. "He didn't really have much more of an ambition for the research other than that." As Rob began this research, it was clear that their data collection methodology, which was essentially poring over newspapers, was extremely flawed and time-consuming. When the professor left the university soon after, the project kind of died with him. Rob went back to researching interest groups in the American political system.

That all changed in the 2001–2 academic year, when Rob returned to Ohio Northern University, this time as a professor. For Rob and his young wife, it was the perfect opportunity to get closer to home, so that they could be near family. Former workers at a spark plug factory, Rob's parents lived nearby Ada. "Even with everyone I have ever met in academia, my parents are some of the smartest people I have ever met," Rob comments with a hint of pride in his voice. Although Rob and his sister are the only ones out of a large extended family that completed a four-year degree (none of his grandparents got more than an eighth-grade education), he shares that his mother had an opportunity to pursue her education but dropped out so that she could take care of her ailing father. Noting that his in-laws also lived nearby, Rob chimes in that he married his high-school sweetheart, who he took to senior prom.

"When I was an undergraduate, I was a member of the political science honor society, Pi Sigma Alpha, at Ohio Northern University. You know, it was just something that you do and you don't really think twice about it," Rob comments. "Well, when I became a faculty member, all of the sudden I found this Pi Sigma Alpha book on my desk and I saw that they had all of these resources that I could use as a professor." One of the resources available was a chapter activity grant.

It was just after the 2000 presidential election and the Electoral College was still a pretty hot topic. Rob began to think of the research question that had been presented to him all those years ago as a graduate student: Who exactly were the electors? He started to think about the possibility of making it a project for Pi Sigma Alpha and applying for a grant. But first, he needed to see if the research had already been done. He got a copy of the Holy Grail of the Electoral College, Yale University Press's *The Electoral College Primer 2000* by Professor Lawrence D. Longley of Wisconsin's Lawrence University and syndicated columnist Neal R. Pierce. Much to his surprise, there was only one page dedicated to explaining who the electors of the Electoral College were.

The wording struck Rob as extremely intriguing. "They wrote something along the lines that the electors were are all 'probably political hacks and fat cats.' They came to the conclusion by finding the photos of electors across the country and seeing that they predominately white males," Rob remembers. He thought there might be fertile ground in the research topic, because nobody seemed to know exactly who the electors even were.

"I told my students that when you are trying to find out something that nobody knows, it is actually really important," Rob comments, remembering having to sell the students a little bit on the research topic. When he discovered that they had received a Pi Sigma Alpha chapter activity grant, Rob was initially a bit worried. He had a sinking feeling in his heart that he had pushed his students too hard into a topic that they weren't even interested in and that he was going to be left having to do all of the work on a massive project. But to his surprise, every single student showed up and jumped into the research process.

"At first, all we were trying to do was to put an actual face to the Electoral College, figuring out who these people were and if they were really 'political hacks and fat cats,'" Rob remembers. They developed a survey and used the chapter activity grant funding to cover paper, printing, and postage. The process of sending out a survey was surprisingly difficult. "There was no ground that had ever been plowed in the field before; we didn't know how to go about even the simple things. We could get the names of the electors, but how could we get the addresses? My students had to become sleuths."

By the time the survey was sent out, Rob was already extremely proud of his students, describing their work as "graduate level research." What Rob was completely unprepared for, however, was the massive response rate that the survey would generate. "The average response rate to a mail survey is something like 20%," Rob comments. "We got a ridiculous response rate: 63% of the electors of the 2000 Electoral College sent their surveys back to us."

As Rob flipped through the surveys, he was surprised by what they looked like. A lot of people took it upon themselves to write comments

Florida and the 2000 Electoral College

Texas Governor George Bush

Vice-President Al Gore

FL

Without Florida, neither candidate had enough Electoral College votes to secure the presidency.

25 VOTES

270
needed to win

BUSH (R)

GORE (D)

| 246 votes pleged | | 267 votes pleged |

538 Total Electoral College Votes

Key Dates:

November 7 – General election day
November 8 – Gore does not recognize Bush as winner due to Florida's close margins
November 26 – Florida declares Bush winner by 537 votes without formal recount
December 12 – *Bush v. Gore* is decided in the Supreme Court, ending hopes for a recount
December 13 – Gore formally concedes the election to Bush
December 18 – The Electoral College votes; Bush gets 271 votes

FLORIDA'S POPULAR VOTE:
BUSH: 2,912,790 votes
GORE: 2,912,253 votes

Bush won Florida by less than 0.01% of the 5,963,110 votes cast

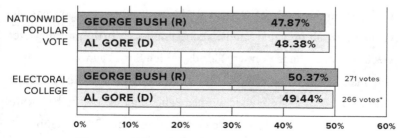

NATIONWIDE POPULAR VOTE

GEORGE BUSH (R) — 47.87%
AL GORE (D) — 48.38%

ELECTORAL COLLEGE

GEORGE BUSH (R) — 50.37% — 271 votes
AL GORE (D) — 49.44% — 266 votes*

0% 10% 20% 30% 40% 50% 60%

There was a faithless elector who did not vote for Gore.

and opinions about the Electoral College in the margins of the survey. Their comments piqued Rob's intellectual curiosity, alongside that of his students. Some people wrote things like "Never again will I serve as an elector" or "I received so many death threats" or "People sent me emails that gave my computer a virus." Rob realized that there was much more to learn about the Electoral College besides just its demographics. Some electors even called Rob at his office, asking him more about his research and offering additional information about their own experiences. Rob admits that a few were skeptical and afraid that he was trying to do research that would lead to the eradication of the Electoral College, but most of the electors who reached out just wanted to have someone to talk to about their experience.

The results of the survey are what really blew Rob away, though. Answers to several questions were especially surprising: Do you believe that George W. Bush was elected legitimately? Was the Florida election legitimate? While 99% of the Republican electors said that Bush was indeed elected legitimately, Rob was shocked by four deviant responses: two Republican electors said that they did not believe that he was elected legitimately and another two said that they weren't sure either way. Two of the four electors hailed from the disputed state of Florida. In other words, these electors could have completely changed the outcome of the election if they had given into their doubts about the President-elect.

The 2000 election was a contentious one that brought the Electoral College into the spotlight. Democrat Al Gore had privately conceded to George W. Bush, only to rescind his concession early in the morning after election night. The reason was Florida, which Bush had won by a razor-thin margin, and its 25 Electoral College votes—which would determine who would be the nationwide winner. Believing the votes to be within a margin of error, Gore demanded a formal recount. On November 26, when Florida said that Bush had won by 537 votes (less than 0.01% of the over 5.9 million votes cast in Florida) without doing a recount, Gore's supporters doubled down and decided to ask for a recount through the court system. On December 12, the Supreme Court said that Florida's recounting mechanisms were rife with equal protection violations, rendering the recount unconstitutional and ensuring Bush the victory.

With the official results of the presidential election hung up for nearly a month, Americans began to question the Electoral College system on a large scale. Al Gore had won the popular vote, garnering 48.4% of the vote and over 540,000 more votes than Bush. The Electoral College also left the country in a perilous situation towards Inauguration Day. Bush was set to win 271 votes (only one vote to spare from the 270 majority votes necessary to win the election) to Gore's pledged 267 votes. Academics realized that if only two members of the Electoral College defected from Bush, it would deny Bush the majority to win and throw the election into the House of Representatives, according to the Twelfth Amendment to the Constitution. The situation was ripe for faithless electors.

Indeed, there was a faithless elector in 2000, but she happened to be a Democrat, not a Republican. Barbara Lett-Simmons, an African American educator and civil rights activist, decided that she was not going to vote for Al Gore the way her hometown of Washington, D.C. had voted. Instead of voting for the Gore/Lieberman ticket, she turned in a blank ballot as a form of protest, saying, "I think that it is an opportunity for us [Washington, D.C.] to make blatantly clear our colonial status and the fact that we've been under an oligarchy."

According to *The Washington Post*, which reported the vote, "Simmons addressed the assembled audience as 'fellow colonists,' and called the treatment of District residents 'immoral, unethical, absolutely wrong and unjust.' The only proper remedy, she said, is for the District to have two voting representatives in the House and two members in the U.S. Senate." Apparently, she also encouraged D.C. residents to stop paying federal taxes during her address. That being said, Lett-Simmons apparently did not see herself as a "faithless elector," commenting that her blank ballot did not count as "faithless." She also told news outlets that if her vote truly mattered in whether or not Gore would win, that she would have voted for Gore without any questions asked.

As Rob perused his results, he realized that the two respondents who believed that the election was illegitimate and the other two who were not sure could have swung the results of the 2000 election as faithless electors. Of course, he recognized the limitations to his research; the timing was far from ideal. He and his students had sent out the surveys in 2003, long after the 2000 vote. He realized that the Republican electors might have gotten increasingly disillusioned with Bush as time went on, perhaps swaying their answers. They also might have discovered new information after the fact that made them question the legitimacy of Bush's win, but that ultimately would have had no impact on their voting whatsoever. Regardless, it was clear that there was a level of unease and distrust. "What that first survey did was remind me that the Electoral College was made up of real human beings," Rob comments. "Everyday people cast their votes to elect George W. Bush into office and these people even sometimes questioned themselves."

Rob claims that it was a bonding experience between him and his students—that they would get equally excited when a new survey got mailed back to them. Every day, students visited him when the mail arrived, hoping that his mailbox was overflowing with returned surveys. "It was very clearly research in action and we were learning things that nobody else knew," Rob remembers. "I wanted to leverage it, so I decided to host an event on campus, inviting some electors from the 2000 election that

I had interacted with through the process." Planned close to the 2004 election night, the event began to attract more and more attention, to the point that CSPAN came out to film it. It was a very big deal for a small university in Ohio. For Rob, it was especially nerve-racking considering that his wife was heavily pregnant with their third child. As he considered everything that could possibly go wrong during the event, his wife's water breaking was one of them.

Rob had handpicked two Democrats and two Republicans from 2000 to join them. On the Republican side, there was a radio host from Missouri and a local Republican grandma from Ohio. "Everybody just loved her," Rob remembers. "On her resume, she had written that she was a home-maker and a baker of a great apple pie. When asked how she got to be an elector, she told everyone that she didn't come from money and she didn't have a fancy last name, she just showed up and worked whenever the Republican Party needed her. She completely negated the 'political hacks and fat cats' stereotype." After Rob's baby girl was born, the Ohio grandma even stopped by the university, bringing a stuffed animal as a gift for the newborn.

The Democratic electors were equally interesting. One Maryland elector was friends with the governor and was kind enough to offer one of Rob's students, who was showing him around, a summer internship. The Pennsylvania elector was a fascinating character with a thick, southern drawl. When Rob first received a phone call from him, he thought that he was talking to an elector from the Deep South and was truly perplexed to find out that he was a Pennsylvania elector. "I asked him how he got to be an elector," Rob recalls, "And he asked me, 'Don't you know? The nominee picks the Pennsylvania electors directly. I was picked by the Gore campaign.'" It turns out that his thick accent came from Arkansas and that he was a childhood friend of Bill Clinton.

The event, which was a resounding success (the Democrats and the Republicans didn't argue at all, even though it was close to the election), made Rob know that he needed to continue his research. He got another Pi Sigma Alpha grant to cover the 2004, 2008, 2012, and 2016 electors, each time honing the survey to get more and more revealing results. Yet, in spite of the fascinating things he knew he was discovering about the Electoral College, he found publishers unwilling to take a chance on his research, opting for more relevant topics than an event that just took place once every four years.

"I would get back reviews saying something along the lines of, 'This is among the most fascinating things I have read in the past year, but we are going to pass because it seems like such a remote topic,'" Rob almost bitterly comments. After nearly a decade of doing surveys, Rob finally got a bite in 2012 and *Presidential Electors and the Electoral College: An Examination of Lobbying, Wavering Electors, and Campaigns for Faithless Votes* was published by Cambria Press. He was proud of himself, but still felt like the research deserved more thought and attention. Little did he know that an election was coming that would put his research on the forefront of the political spin news cycle.

Levi Guerra
Part 2

L.J. Guerra had begun to feel more and more uncomfortable with being an elector in the Electoral College as the summer went on. In her speech at the Congressional Caucus, where she was chosen from over 60 candidates, she had said that she was going to represent the people in her district and her community through her Electoral College vote. "As things went along in the caucus, it was clear that Sanders had a lot more support from the Democrats in my area than Clinton did," she recalls. To make matters even more complicated for the recently turned 19-year-old, her district often voted Republican. "So, it wasn't like just Democrats weren't very happy with Clinton. The Republicans, who were the majority, weren't happy with Clinton either." For L.J., this predicament just didn't feel right.

However, she didn't really think much about the Electoral College vote until she received an email that instructed her to sign a pledge that she would vote for Hillary Clinton in the Electoral College vote in December. If she didn't sign the paper, the email instructed, she would be subject to removal. If she voted faithlessly the day of, she would be subject to a $1,000 fine. The fine didn't sit well with L.J. In her mind, she had been voted in by her peers; she couldn't believe that her electorship might be taken away from her if she didn't sign a piece of paper.

Once again, L.J. felt like she was put in a position of disadvantage due to her socio-economic background. "It felt like basically what they were saying was that voting what you feel is right is something that is only in reach for wealthy electors, who can pay the $1,000 without thinking twice and be let off the hook." As off-putting as the pledge was, L.J. didn't want to give up her position as an elector, so she signed the pledge. Finding a way to fax it back, though, proved to be a challenge. She eventually went to the library at Big Bend Community College and asked if they had the resources to fax it over. She remembers how her school's librarian kind of chuckled and taught her how to use a fax machine.

L.J. didn't know what to expect out of the Electoral College, but she certainly didn't expect this. "I just kept thinking to myself, why are there actual living human beings in the Electoral College? It just didn't make sense. Why would you have actual humans do this, when all they are essentially doing is acting like a stamp to certify something?" L.J. ponders. "If the purpose of the electors is just to be a stamp, then the electors have no point at all. You could replace us with robots. You could even put a dog in our place, for that matter."

When she got a Facebook message from Bret Chiafalo soon after, asking if she was interested in talking elector-to-elector, she was intrigued and immediately agreed. She felt like she needed to talk all of these ideas and feelings out with someone. To her relief, she claims Bret echoed many of the same concerns. Together, they agreed that they were simply electors and that more qualified individuals, perhaps in the court system, should be addressing these sorts of questions. She hung up with Bret that summer with the idea that she might do something different with her Electoral College vote, but she didn't know what or how.

One thing that she did know: if she was going to do something out of the ordinary, she needed to understand exactly what her rights and responsibilities were. She began to do research about the Electoral College in all her free time. She had so many questions that she didn't know where to start: Had other electors done something unexpected? When? And why? With all of the questions that she had about the Electoral College, she wanted to understand what the intentions of the Founding Fathers were. She borrowed a copy of The Federalist Papers from one of her employers and read about how Hamilton had described that the electors could be the last line of defense against a potential tyrant. "The more I looked into the topic of the Founding Fathers, the more strongly I felt that this was not a question that I should be answering," she states. "I was not capable of determining what the intentions of the Founding Fathers were. But someone with the ability to interpret that should definitely be answering these questions." She began to feel more and more strongly that Bret Chiafalo had the right idea—trying to introduce this topic into the United States court system.

At the same time, the idea of paying a $1,000 fine was absolutely frightening to L.J., who was unsure of how she would be able to afford it. After she turned eighteen, she knew that she could have moved out on her own, but had decided to live at home so that she could help her family. She knew that nobody in her immediate family had the extra money to spare. "Did it take a lot of bravery for me to say that I didn't care about the fine, that I was going to do what I believed was right? Yes, for sure," L.J. remembers. "Did it scare the hell out of me that I might have to pay the fine anyway? Yes. Do I think that I would have done anything differently? No."

Elected as a Democratic elector by people who didn't seem to be very enthusiastic about Clinton, L.J wasn't exactly sure what to do. What was right and wrong didn't seem so cut-and-dry or straightforward, so she decided to take things into her own hands. Late that summer, L.J. created her own straw polls and started going around to different areas in the community to ask people, if they could make up their own ideal presidential candidate, what sort of characteristics might that candidate have.

She mostly hung out at two of the local Wal-Marts, as well as some local mom-and-pop grocery stores, and approached people to ask if they would participate in her survey. As they answered her questions, she diligently took notes. "It is really funny to me now," L.J. chuckles to herself, "I didn't say or do anything wrong; but I was such a different person back then. The military changed me. I remember just being petrified going up to people trying to start these conversations. I was not confident at all."

Through her straw polls, L.J. developed a list of qualities that she thought her constituents wanted in a President. "Most people in my community wanted someone with military experience. They wanted someone who was respected by Democrats and Republicans alike. And they also wanted someone who valued the importance of education," L.J. rambles off the list. Once she had the list, she began to do research to determine who would be the best person who checked off all three of the boxes. She put some keywords in the Google search bar and very quickly General Colin Powell's name came up. As she looked into Colin Powell's background, she knew that this was the type of person that her constituents would want. She had the candidate that was worth the risk of having to pay the $1,000 fine.

L.J. was going about doing all of the research on her own; it didn't really dawn on her that there were others across the country who were actively studying the Electoral College. She remembers telling one of her professors the semester before that she had been chosen as an elector and wanted to talk about it, but her professor simply did not believe her and the conversations went nowhere. A bit crushed by the rejection, she decided that she would do all of the research and straw polls by herself, following her own instinct.

The General Election results didn't surprise L.J.; she had a feeling that Donald Trump might win. However, what did surprise her was the amount of interest in the Electoral College that suddenly appeared after Trump won. "I really don't think that people would have cared about the Electoral College and the questions that I felt needed to be to addressed if Clinton had won," L.J. notes. She quickly began to realize that people were starting to view the Electoral College as a last-ditch effort to keep Trump out of the White House. While that wasn't necessarily her personal motivation or intention, she was just pleased that people were finally starting to pay attention to what the Electoral College was.

One of her former high school teachers reached out to her once she discovered that L.J. was an elector. L.J. was shocked by her teacher's comments. "She told me that she never before in her entire life had met an elector," L.J. recalls. "Here she was, with a doctorate in history, never having met an elector. She told me that she didn't even know if electors really existed; let alone if they could be ordinary people."

L.J. got a lot of positive reinforcement from this teacher, who seemed to understand what L.J. was wanting to do by bringing attention to the Electoral College system and demanding that the court system come up with answers about the rights of electors. "Most people—and that is if they know anything about the Electoral College at all (a lot of people don't)—will ask you a question like: Do you agree with the Electoral College? Or do you not agree with the Electoral College?" L.J. remembers, finding this paradigm of viewing the Electoral College system extremely frustrating. "To me, that is not the question that we should be asking."

Even though L.J. was still extremely afraid of public speaking, she was convinced by Bret and the growing Hamilton Electors movement to give a speech on the steps of the Washington State Capitol, stating her intent not to vote for Clinton. L.J. was willing to do anything that she needed to do at the time to get the movement up-and-running.

"I didn't realize that the press conference was going to be such a big deal," L.J. comments. "I cannot watch the video of my speech for so many reasons. The first being that I still have no idea what I was thinking when I put on that outfit that morning." She remembers a lot going through her mind. She wasn't sure what the result of her speech would be; but she was determined to do her absolute best. She reminded herself that her goal was just to get people talking about the Electoral College.

And talk they did. L.J. scoffs at many of the comments that she reads on the internet now, especially the conspiracy theories about her. She thinks that a lot of the comments were stemming from the fact that she was a woman and people believe that women are more easily manipulatable than men. She remembers a post of her friend on Facebook, linking to Levi's speech. "Clearly someone didn't connect the dots and realize that this was a friend posting about her friend," she remembers. "A guy commented, 'How the hell does a little girl become an elector?'" At first, L.J. was a bit irked by the comment; but then she realized that this was exactly the dialogue and questions that she was trying to bring up with her Electoral College vote.

The more she thought about the comments on the internet, the more she felt like she had made the right decision. "People need to ask questions," she says. "I wanted Americans to see what the Electoral College is in today's era, not what it was, and not what it was supposed to be, but what it actually is. I wanted them to ask what role the Electoral College would end up playing in 2016. I wanted them to ask what role the Electoral College would play in 2020."

Even so, L.J. started slowly taking herself off social media; it was a lot for her to handle, all while she was working two different jobs. But the public wasn't going to let her off so easily. Her speech had unleashed a new strain of conspiracy theorists, who were intent on placing her within their warped view of society. She started to receive death threats in the mail. Some people sent her letters outlining their crazy conspiracy theories and trying to figure out where she fit in them. "My parents responded to the death threats with a sense of humor," L.J. comments, "My father was a former marine and I don't think he was scared at all." The letters sat there; the family didn't share them with law enforcement. Her mother later just packed them away along with L.J.'s other things, like school report cards and class projects.

Micheal Baca
Part 3

Micheal Baca was flying over to Texas, where he was going to laud the first big break of the fledgling Hamilton Electors: they had a Republican elector named Chris Suprun willing to say on the record that he wasn't planning on voting for Trump. Micheal had decided that one of his strongest suits and his favorite parts about the Hamilton Electors was the media. He was getting increasingly comfortable in front of a camera. He wasn't that close to his family, but a lot of them would watch his CNN interviews. One of his uncles even called up afterwards with tips ("you can't interrupt so much" and "you need to listen with the intention to understand, not the intention to respond"), advice which Micheal has tried to follow ever since.

His old Marine friends also wrote in saying that they had seen Micheal on television. "Most of them are on the conservative end of the spectrum," he laughs, "They kept sending me over names of people that they thought I should vote for instead of Trump—mostly Ron Paul and Rand Paul." Of course, his appearances also brought about a certain amount of infamy. Micheal started getting death threats sent anonymously to his Facebook account. Others who had announced that they stood with the Hamilton electors—including some Colorado Democrats who followed in Micheal's footsteps—were starting to get scared and feel unsafe. Micheal remembers that someone had their tires slashed. On the advice of a journalist friend, he referred all his death threats to the FBI.

Micheal also started to get the feeling that his technology was compromised. Always on his phone's GPS as a part-time Uber driver, Micheal started to get strange phone calls. "The phone was definitely ringing, but it was blank. I would pick it up but there was nothing. I could not call the number back." With blank phone calls filling up his Caller ID (some of which lasted minutes), Micheal started to worry. Once he started talking to political operatives, he was surprised how careful everyone was to only share information on encrypted platforms, a habit which he also started to adopt.

Micheal's time in Dallas was a whirlwind. He wasn't in Texas for more than 24 hours and most of that was just with Chris Suprun's lawyer. There were three or four major news networks with their cameras covering the event. Micheal agreed with major initiatives like press conferences; he was getting increasingly irked with the Hamilton Electors' pro-bono Mr. D, who suggested that they take a grassroots approach with local candlelight vigils.

In Micheal's mind, they were wasting a lot of money on small-scale initiatives. "Once money got involved, things just got weird. I felt like contracts were just being put up in my face and people were telling me to 'sign this' and 'sign that.' At one point we had $300,000 in the bank. And even though I was President and spending all of this time working on it, I wasn't getting paid and was just barely making ends meet with my two jobs," Micheal comments. He saw the money dwindle as more and more checks were written out to strategy and communication consultants. At the same time, Micheal doesn't complain; he knows that a huge amount of the publicity that they were getting was precisely because they had hired these individuals and groups.

Another challenge facing the Hamilton Electors, according to Micheal, was that they were not the only ones who realized that the election could be swayed by faithless electors. A Change.Org petition asking Republican electors to switch their votes to Clinton in honor of the popular vote quickly got over 5 million signatures. Inspired after realizing that Trump could lose the presidency after all, people around the country began creating websites and blog posts, sharing contact information for the Republican electors. Within two weeks after the general vote, the Republican electors had been completely bombarded and were unwilling to be in contact with yet another organization. "I think that these people went about it the wrong way; they created an argument that would never convince Republicans," Micheal stipulates. "Trump losing the popular vote doesn't matter. The rules were there, and Trump won the presidency according to the rules. We all knew it was like this. George W. Bush won the same way in 2000."

"I felt like we didn't have the luxury of wasting any time trying to ally with a group that didn't totally fit with our message and strategy," Micheal says. However, as multiple groups had their own separate agendas, the messaging inevitably got mixed up in the minds of the electors, as well as the public. Conservative media started to claim that so many groups and initiatives was an indication of a massive liberal conspiracy to rob Trump of the presidency—a claim that was seemingly confirmed when liberal movie producer Michael Moore offered (unprompted) to pay any legal fees that Republican electors might incur if they voted for someone other than Donald Trump. But honestly speaking, sometimes the Hamilton Electors found themselves helping out some of these other organizations, feeding off each other's resources and momentum. One such example was the Hamilton Electors' promotion of Unite for America's content, including a video that featured *The West Wing* actor Martin Sheen describing the Electoral College as the last line of defense for keeping Trump out of office.

But Micheal had a new radical plot forming in his head: Knowing that Bill Clinton was an elector for the state of New York, he thought that if Bill Clinton voted against his wife for a more moderate Republican and Hillary publicly unbound her electors, Republicans would feel confident that they could also vote their conscience—which he assumed would be against Trump. "My thought was that if we could get someone large enough, why not just shoot for the moon?" Micheal remembers, almost wistfully. "Getting Bill Clinton as a Hamilton Elector would make major waves." Micheal pitched the idea to some Clinton advisers in a closed-door, hush-hush meeting around Thanksgiving. He left the meeting feeling positive that his idea would at least be considered, and was extremely frustrated when he never heard back.

Before long, however, Micheal was back to his role in the public eye, rather than power-brokering behind the scenes: He was in DC for a press conference with Chris Suprun, trying to rally up support for the Hamilton Electors. "It was more or less a regular march; about 800 to 1,000 of us marched around Pennsylvania Avenue and held up candles in some purple cups." It was his second time ever in Washington, D.C. and he was still a bit in awe, feeling so close and relevant to these bodies of power. "I was inspired by the place. I was inspired just by being there. I could see the Washington Monument; to the left, I could see the Lincoln Memorial;

and to my right, I could see the Capitol." He was surprised by the crowd, which was large enough to fill up one of the streets.

However, as the event drew to a close, he realized that he didn't know anyone who had shown up for the protest, so he went to eat by himself at a restaurant. While in Washington, perhaps still irked by the Clintons' disregard of his plan for Hillary to unbind her electors, he came up with a new, big idea: He had just signed his name to fellow Electoral College member Christine Pelosi's letter to Director of National Intelligence James Clapper, demanding information about allegations of Russian interference in the presidential election. If he couldn't get a Clinton to join the Hamilton Electors, perhaps he could get a Pelosi to join one. He came up with the idea of doing a protest in front of the White House, where all the Hamilton Electors would demand information about Russia. "I thought it would be very powerful," he comments, "But this idea just fell on deaf ears. Instead, my team just kept putting all of this time and energy into those candlelight vigils."

Art Sisneros
Part 3

S ometimes Art Sisneros wonders if his biggest mistake was that he was
going through his own unique process of self-discovery as an elector
during the same 2016 presidential election cycle that "liberals were target-
ing electors to switch the vote." The normal, unspoken rules that seemed
to dictate previous elections had changed: liberals were becoming strict
Constitutionalists, alluding to Alexander Hamilton as they attempted to
get Republicans to switch their vote, while Republicans simply said that
they wanted Art to do his job and duty as an elector.

"Conservatives turned schizophrenic," Art comments. "They say they
want a republic, but they ultimately want the mob rule of democracy."
Describing their treatment of the Constitution like a taxi, Art believes
that conservatives were only wanting to take the Constitution as far as

they wanted to go and then hop off. To Art, the Constitution didn't work that way. He had been researching the Electoral College for months before he wrote his "Biblical Voting in the Age of Trump" blog post that would end up going viral. Instead of delving into his personal thought process as an elector, he wanted this post to inspire reflection about the moral implications of voting as a Christian, as well as the type of government that the United States has.

However, once the Hamilton Electors began to gain steam, people quickly connected the dots and targeted him as a potential faithless elector. If given the chance, Art admits that he would have gone back and rewritten a few things to clarify his position—he just had no way of expecting the outside pressure he would soon be under.

"A lot of people started messaging me, even people in the Liberty Movement, saying that I was supporting a theocracy in my blog post and reminding me about the separation of church and state," Art remembers. "I would have clarified two issues. The first is that there is an Electoral College set up for electors to vote for who they believe would be the best candidate. The second is that, because of my faith, I believe that Donald Trump was not the best candidate and I would not vote for him."

Art knew that he was in a bit of a pickle when he reached out to three older men whose opinions he truly cherished, asking them for advice. When they gave three completely separate pieces of advice, Art realized that this was a journey that he would ultimately have to make alone. Art remembers being touched as his friends, church community, and coworkers rallied to support him, even if they didn't all agree with his decision. He believes that he got so much support because his friends respected him. They knew that when he decided to do something, that he had put a lot of thought, research, and effort into that decision. Tongue-in-cheek, he also admits that he can be pretty stubborn and that maybe his friends knew that they had absolutely no chance of changing his mind once it was set.

Acquaintances and strangers did try to change Art's opinions about voting for Trump, however. "They would try to question me and I would counter them with questions like: 'Why should electors even vote in the Electoral College? Should the Electoral College be erased then? Do you think that we should have complete democracy, rather than a republic? Do you think I personally should not vote my conscience according to what the Bible says? Do you think that Trump is biblically qualified to be President?'" Art remembers that most of them didn't have any answers to his questions, but ended the conversations by reminding him that Hillary Clinton was "the worst." While he might agree with the statement, that wasn't the issue that Art was trying to address, so he mostly ignored them.

One thing that Art could not ignore, however, was the threats that he and his family had started to receive. Sometimes, he had a hard time concentrating at work, knowing that his wife and children were sitting at home alone, homeschooling. He tried to assure himself that somebody who was serious about a threat of that magnitude wouldn't post it on Facebook or send a letter with a return address. He felt additionally secure with the knowledge that he and his wife were conceal-carriers of firearms, so they would be able to protect themselves if anything happened. Many of the threats were a bit surprising to Art, especially when they came from people who said that they were Christians. Someone who claimed to be a pastor threatened him, saying that he had former military experience and had sworn an oath to uphold the Constitution. Art didn't know what to say—in his mind, he was acting in accordance to his constitutional rights. Eventually, he and his wife started throwing all the letters into a box by the door and began to throw them away, without even reading them.

Arguments in favor of voting for Trump were like a bug in his ear, however, and he didn't know what to do about it. "People started saying that I needed to vote for Trump because I had signed a pledge. And I realized that was not entirely untrue. I had indeed signed a pledge and, in my opinion, a pledge is important," Art comments. In his defense, he describes the pledge process as chaotic and seemingly lacking in importance. "Basically, all of the people who were chosen to be electors were asked to stand in a line in front of a table before we left the State Convention. Once we got to the front of the line, there were these pledges printed out on sheets of paper and we were just supposed to sign our names." While Art vaguely knew that there was a pledge, he never saw the wording until after he had been elected by his peers, which diminished its validity a bit in his mind. He was also irked that there was no one there to witness him signing the pledge.

Art claims that he didn't know what he was signing himself up for when he ran for elector. He also had a feeling that the delegates at the State Convention who elected him didn't understand the roles and responsibilities of the elector position either, which worried him. He understood that technically he could vote for whomever he wanted as an elector, as set forth by the Constitution. He was worried that perhaps the people who put him in that elector position to start with didn't understand that he could vote his personal conscience. Besides that, there was the pledge that he had to deal with. Somebody suggested that since the pledge's vague wording to support the presidential and the vice-presidential nominees left a lot to be desired, Art could actually just switch the two, voting Mike Pence for President and Donald Trump for Vice-President. Art thought it was an interesting premise, but also understood that it didn't quite honor the intent of the oath which he signed.

As Art's blog post began to get more and more attention, he realized that a light was shining on him, providing an opportunity to be an example of a person faithful to God, noting that "all that I tried to do was not bring shame to Christ." As he thought about what the right course of action was, he began to think that stepping down might be the most honorable thing. He hadn't considered it before the general election, but after being reminded of his pledge, he felt strongly that it might be the best option. He sat down and began to write a second blog post, "Conflicted Elector in a Corrupt College," a 2,500-word essay that sorted through his personal struggles, noting that in regard to the pledge:

> It was a voluntary pledge and I willingly signed it. I was wrong in signing this pledge and not communicating to the body when I ran that my conscience would not be bound by it. I honestly did not have the convictions about the original purpose of the Electoral College or the biblical qualifications until after I was an Elector. The Bible calls this a rash oath and warns against making them. It clearly states,
>
> "if a person swears, speaking thoughtlessly with his lips to do evil or good, whatever it is that a man may pronounce by an oath, and he is unaware of it- when he realizes it, then he shall be guilty in any of these matters. And it shall be, when he is guilty in any of these matters, that he shall confess that he has sinned in that thing." [Leviticus 5:4,5]

He posted the blog post on The Blessed Path on November 26 and went on The Liberty Line podcast to publicly reconfirm his decision to step down. Noting that there was no provision for an elector-elect like himself to resign, he said that by coming out publicly, he was letting the Texas Republican Party know about his resignation. Afterwards, Art felt an overwhelming sense of relief. He was sure that the Trump supporters would finally get off his back and that the liberals would move on to their next target.

But instead, the attention focused on him ramped up even more, with the second article getting even more attention than the first. Even though his mind was already made up, he was constantly getting contacted by people who thought that they could change it. He was messaged by media outlets from all around the world, wanting to come to his office and his home with a big camera crew. "This wasn't about me or seeing my face in the press," Art comments, noting that he had already moved on and was now thinking about preparing for Christmas with his growing brood of children. "I was really uncomfortable with that. So, when I got these requests, I just pointed them to my article. I guessed that if people are not willing to read something, they are just going to hear what they want to hear."

Art was already tuning all the craziness out when he got a call from the Chairman of the Texas Republican Party, seemingly wanting to confirm that he indeed was planning on giving up his electorship. Instead of engaging him in conversation, Art sent him his blog posts and said that he was looking forward to discussing them with him. When he didn't get a response, he wasn't surprised (having always had perhaps a bit of a beef with the establishment Republicans), but was slightly disappointed. Although, he prefaced talking about this interaction with the party leadership with, "I have never been very good about taking orders from anybody," Art didn't have any tricks up his sleeve. When the Electoral College vote occurred on December 19 at the Texas State House, Art was nowhere to be found. The Texas Republican Party replaced him with another pre-approved candidate, who unsurprisingly voted for Trump.

At the time, Art was fine about giving up his future in the Republican Party, which he publicly said on his friends' podcast. However, a few years later, he admits that the Electoral College actually ended up having a major impact on his political engagement. "I pay attention to politics now, but I am not that active anymore," he admits. "I feel like I kind of lost my voice in this process. But I don't complain because I am seeing that as my boys get older, they need me more and more. I need to be home for them." His limited political role was clearly determined through trial-and-error, however. He noted that after the Electoral College, it was a bit taboo for him to show up to any local political events, even to the Abolition Abortion group that he helped start. "It became clear that if I didn't show up and just supported from the sidelines, that it was better for the movement." While this likely hurt, Art doesn't dwell on it, noting, "this was never about me anyway and many more people across the world have suffered far worse for standing up for their beliefs."

Noting that his faith is what made him come to his decision to give up his place in the Electoral College, he despises the term of the faithless elector. "I am actually a faithful elector," Art stipulates passionately. To him the term faithless elector is an oxymoron; a nonsensical term that has nothing to do with the roles and responsibilities of the office. "It is a derogatory term for sure, and that is not by accident. They want you to think that you are supposed to do what they want you to do," he notes, without defining exactly who "they" are.

In hindsight, Art wishes that he might have done things a bit differently, noting that he was never a formal elector because he didn't show up to the December 19 vote. Throughout this whole process, he was only an elector-elect. Although he claims that he really wasn't sure what to expect when he first signed up to be an elector, he imagines and describes to me a reality in which he had. "I would have made it clear from the very beginning that I was intending on voting my conscience. If the delegates knew and voted me in anyway, I would have been fine signing the pledge and disregarding it on the voting day," he envisions. He does wish that his Electoral College vote could have counted, as he believes that it might have brought attention to the political issues that truly mattered to him. When I ask, he even has a shortlist of candidates that he would have considered, including Ron Paul and Texas legislators David Simpson and Jonathan Strickland.

However, Art doesn't regret anything, believing that he made a difference regardless. "Two years later, a friend of mine got elected as a Texas State House representative and called me from the floor of the House saying that he had just filed a bill for the freedom of electors in my honor," Art recalls with pride. He knew that the bill didn't have any shot at passing, but felt a certain emotion knowing that people had been watching his personal struggle and were moved by it. "Most people don't feel the privilege of having public pressure from the outside," he comments.

Art believes that most importantly, he acted as a positive example for his children, teaching them how to wrestle with difficult ethical choices as a Christian, when the choices aren't so cut-and-dry. "This experience has made me realize that I need to start viewing a lot of the decisions I make on a day-to-day basis with the same thought and care that I did the Electoral College. I am trying to be more self-aware of my actions, because I only realized after the fact that so many people were watching me to see what I would do next."

Some of Art's favorite conversations were the ones he had with strangers from the opposite political spectrum, many of whom were trying in vain to convince him to stay on as an elector to vote against Trump. Noting that they actually had a lot more common ground than the conservative and liberal media would like them to believe that they had, he said that his conversations with this group of people were some of the most intellectually fulfilling and enriching. "Some liberal atheists told me that they grew up in Christian homes and have since left the faith," he remembers. "When they saw family and friends being hypocritical, doing things that were not in line with what they said they believed, they thought that their faith wasn't real. A few people have said that if they knew more people like me, who lived out the convictions they said they believed in, they may not have left." These were the only words that Art needed to hear to know that, in spite of all of the political reper- cussions and getting pushed out of the Republican Party, he had made the right choice.

The Novelist

In 2015, James McCrone followed his wife to Oxford University, where she had accepted a one-year appointment as a visiting fellow in American constitutional law. It was certainly a transition year: their three kids were already out of the house and while his wife had a work permit for the United Kingdom, James did not. Instead of complaining about it, he decided to turn it into something positive: the stint abroad would be the perfect opportunity to finally do what he had been dreaming of since he was twelve years old: writing his own political thriller.

He found an editor through the Oxford community and began to think about which of his projects that he most wanted to materialize. He had received a Master of Fine Arts in creative writing from the University of Washington in Seattle; but instead of a fully-formed novel, he had been focusing mostly on short stories. "It was time that I finished my first novel," the now 56-year-old laughs, "Or else I would need to quit calling myself a writer!"

Going through his old projects, he remembered a very rough manuscript on a political thriller that he had written nearly twenty years prior—in 1996—that had gone absolutely nowhere. In his heart, he had a special place for this book because he had developed the concept all the way back when he was a preteen. His father, a political science professor at the University of Washington in Seattle, was teaching him about how the United States presidential elections worked. "The system sounded mad and so I started asking more and more questions about it," he recalls. "So, as my father was discussing the Electoral College, he began mentioning faithless electors to me." While his father was quick to point out that faithless electors had never actually turned an election, he noted that things could get very interesting in a close election when only a couple of electors would be the difference between winning and losing.

"The idea that a small number of electors could overturn a result really stuck in my mind," James says. "I didn't know what I would do with it at the time, but it seemed intriguing and important." When he turned the scenario into a political thriller in 1996, he was surprised when it didn't gain any traction. However, by the time the 2000 presidential election had come around, he was certain that it would get a lot of interest. Al Gore, Bill Clinton's Vice President, had won the popular vote nationwide while George W. Bush had managed to win the majority of votes in the Electoral College (what political scientists often call a "misfire" election.)

What made the scenario even more complicated was the fact that less than 600 votes separated Bush and Gore in Florida—well within a margin of error, especially when considering miscounted votes or potential voter fraud. If the votes were recounted and it turned out that Gore had won, he would have been the uncontested winner. Although Gore had originally conceded to Bush, by the time election night was over, he had rescinded his concession and demanded a recount.

For a month, the United States was on pins and needles, without knowing for sure who would be the next President, until the Supreme Court stepped in and in a highly contested decision, declared that there would be no recount. While the whole scenario was often overshadowed by debates on the popular vote or judicial authority, what some political scientists were thinking about was the fact that the election itself might easily be decided by a few faithless electors. Indeed, even with Florida, Bush only had a few more electors than Gore. If the election was as hotly contested by electors as it was by the general public, then the presidency might still have been up for grabs.

James thought it represented the perfect opportunity: he was sure that this renewed nationwide interest in the Electoral College might provide the right environment for his political thriller to take off. So, he polished the draft a bit, but it still didn't go anywhere. Literary agents and publishers wrote back to him with positive feedback on his writing style and the characters, but always ended it with something along the lines that no readers were interested in picking up a book about the Electoral College for fun. "Honestly, in that form, it wasn't very good," he admits. "So I just ended up putting it away and not thinking about it for a very, very long time."

"I had the very basic plot—a close election and a group of shadowy provocateurs who want to steal the election for their own ends—but I struggled with how I wanted to tell it." James decided that he would focus on a world that he grew up in and understood—the university community. He starts the novel with a young university researcher, Matthew Yamashita, who is looking into the Electoral College when he discovers that electors are dying at an unprecedented rate.

"You think about it," James tells me with enthusiasm in his voice, "Everything about the Electoral College is just happening state-by-state; nobody is really taking national notes. A conspiracy could only have been discovered by someone like Matthew, who is combing through the data." Indeed, Robert Alexander of Ohio Northern University did a double take when he read the university scenes in James's novel, recalling how his own research often mirrors that of the characters. "One night as we were preparing our research surveys for the electors, my students explained to me how we could all be characters in a thriller," Rob comments. "I couldn't believe that somebody else from the outside could have seen it, too."

When Matthew meets an untimely end, his faculty adviser Duncan Caldwell decides to pick up his crusade to stop unknown villains from fixing the election, calling upon one of his former students (who conveniently works for the FBI), Imogene Trager, to help make it happen. "I have always heard that you should write what you know. In my case, I knew the university," James comments. When I ask if James based the main protagonist, Duncan, on his father, James bursts into laughter. "No, not at all," but then adds facetiously: "Actually, I just might have killed my father off on page 5." One of the electors who is killed by a mysterious cabal early in the book owned a vineyard in Oregon; his father had likewise purchased land in Oregon after his retirement to build a vineyard. "I didn't quite realize I had done that, until some friends started accusing me of killing my father in a literary sense."

Although James had a rough draft already completed, after a few interactions with his editor, he knew that it needed a lot of work. James's editor axed entire sections of the novel, which James describes as extremely painful, but ultimately necessary. However, one of James's biggest challenges was that the world had transformed since he first wrote the book in 1996.

"I remember this one section, when my editor just wrote alongside my pages that he didn't get it. If Matthew thought he needed to tell Duncan something important, why didn't he just use his cell phone to call Duncan? I realized the reason why was that when I first conceptualized this book, we didn't even have cell phones! Can you imagine?"

James knew that he had a window of opportunity during the 2015–6 school year. He decided that he would treat his writing like it was his job, and would sit down to write every day. As the chef of his family, he knew that he had household responsibilities to take care of, too. It took him a while to develop a schedule, but once he did, he was extremely productive. He woke up early alongside his wife, made breakfast and coffee, and saw her out the door before 8 in the morning. He would then go out to the morning markets and buy everything that he planned to fix for the rest of the day. Inevitably, by 10, he would be sitting down at his desk, writing. His wife would return home at 7 P.M. so he would write for hours until it was time to cook to have dinner ready.

By the time he finished another draft and gave it to his editor in December 2015, he wondered what it would take to get it published. He knew that if he found a traditional publisher for it, it wouldn't come out for possibly another two years. For some reason, James felt that there was a time crunch for his book. He began to think about self-publishing, an option that wasn't available to him earlier. "I wanted it to catch some of the excitement and attention that an election year would generate, so I made the decision to self-publish." His editor dutifully polished it up and he found someone to do a powerful piece of cover art: a black, white, red, and blue cover with a big "X" over the state of Illinois. His novel, *Faithless Elector*, came out in March 2016.

James was extremely proud of the book; he felt that it articulated the zeitgeist of the moment. There was a big difference between his book and the Cold War spy thrillers that he grew up reading. "Nowadays, we are realizing that so many problems that are occurring are our fault, not that of an enemy like the Soviet Union," James comments. "We prevailed in the Cold War; but oddly it doesn't feel like a win. We succeeded and our democratic principles and market economy took over the world. But, at home, we are filled with conspiracies, shadows, and rumors. This new, implacable foe is compelling." James thinks that a mysterious cabal that is trying to fix elections by killing off electors and replacing them with electors whom they can control is a better narrative than regurgitating that outsiders are always the enemy, which in his mind, doesn't always go well with our increasingly globalized world.

In spite of James's enthusiasm, not many books were sold in March or April. Self-publishing was proving to be a challenge, because he wasn't sure what distribution vendors to use or how to get the reviews he so desperately needed to get traction. "Even today," he bemoans, "the book is not in the Seattle library. And now I live in Philadelphia and the book isn't in the Philadelphia library either, even though I have asked them to carry it." James takes a localized approach to getting his book picked up by bookstores: printing out flyers, delivering them to bookstores, and offering to give talks or do events.

However, after the National Conventions, James's gut instinct was proven correct, perhaps due to his political background—a factor that he typically downplays. "I was politically engaged starting from a young age, but having a father who is a teacher makes you realize how much you don't know rather than what you do know," James says, noting that many of his political predictions end up being dead wrong. "Once the parties settled on their candidates, everything started to come together. Sales started to go crazy in late June and there was a huge spike of sales toward the end of the year, which carried into 2017."

Of course, James would have never guessed that the faithless electors would have taken on such prominence in that election cycle. It was a bit of a fluke. Even the satirical bellwether Saturday Night Live had an entire skit, where a jilted Hillary Clinton showed up to a Republican elector's house à la holiday classic movie *Love Actually*, trying to convince the elector to vote for her instead of Trump through a series of white posters.

Although James claims that he has no political axe to grind, he admits that he thinks that the Electoral College is "a pretty muddy way to elect our leaders. For there to be so many loopholes is really quite unnerving. For something that is this important and where the stakes are so high, it should be something that the public can understand." As he wrote the book, he found it difficult to find people with whom he could discuss ideas and possibilities (considering that most of the actions that occurred in his book had never happened, he wasn't exactly sure what would happen in certain situations.) For that, he reached out to political scientist Robert Alexander, whose research he relied on and with whom he communicated via email and Twitter.

For a political thriller, James's story is surprisingly apolitical—he purposefully left out actual political figures and people who resembled political figures to "allow readers to focus on the story." He prides himself in having Republican and Democratic fans who have reached out to him on social media, as well as non-citizen fans. ("It meant that I must have done a good job at explaining a pretty complicated system," he gives himself credit.) "As I worked on rewrites, I was careful to craft a story that wasn't a polemic. In my view, people don't read fiction to have the writer tell them what to think."

As I continued to speak with James, one of the things that really stuck with me was how a novelist had become an expert of sorts on faithless electors. Indeed, in an era of social media and a seemingly unlimited amount of information online, novelists, rather than academics or well-known politicos, have been at the forefront of warning voters about the pitfalls of the Electoral College. Roy Neel, a longtime Al Gore staffer, and Jeff Greenfield, a PBS television news contributor, have also both written novels that feature the topic of faithless electors.

Perhaps the possibility of faithless electors seems so far-fetched that most people mistakenly don't take it seriously. Or perhaps the Electoral College is just too complicated to feature in a blockbuster. Or perhaps each party is nervous about exposing the vulnerabilities of the Electoral College system, fearing that doing so might benefit the other. Regardless, the result is the same: faithless electors is a topic generally overlooked by even the country's most politically-savvy.

When writing his book, James was incredibly careful not to let his political opinions take center stage, a quality that he likely learned from growing up with politics being viewed as an academic subject, rather than something to argue about around the dinner table. When I ask him what his motivation was for writing the story, he avoids a didactic answer: "This book was a true labor of love, a passion. I wanted to write a page-turning thriller with strong characters and a dramatic premise that was believable enough to be disquieting. I believe I did that."

David Mulinix
Part 2

D avid Mulinix was in a bit of a conundrum—he was now an elector for the state of Hawaii in the Electoral College, but when he started to think deeply about it, he didn't want to be an elector at all. "The Founding Fathers thought that there were too many uneducated people in the country who couldn't possibly vote, so they created this system to keep them from having political empowerment," he exclaims.

But in the next few sentences, David begins to show an aspect of his personality that has infused the vast majority of our conversations: Although he has strong opinions about politics and society, he is willing to consider the other side of the aisle, too. "Maybe I give the Founding Fathers too hard of a time," he comments. "Sure, they were old, rich white guys. But at the same time, they had progressive ideas for that era. They would come together to meet and study. They were committed to seeing the world in a different way." He begins to share with me questions that he would ask Thomas Jefferson if provided the chance, imagining what he would have felt meeting him in person.

After some back-and-forth, David comes down to the real reason that he is uncomfortable with the Electoral College system: he didn't like the idea that he could override the popular vote. "There were only four of us in the Electoral College in Hawaii," he comments. "I don't like that the four of us could have met up beforehand and decided who we were going to vote for and essentially overridden everyone else's votes. There is something wrong with that."

Simultaneously, David was facing a personal challenge of party loyalty, knowing full well that many expected him to represent the will of the Democratic Party through his electorship. "I think that we might need a 'none of the above' box to check on the ballot. Sometimes, the options on that list … I simply cannot vote for those people," he comments. Although he is now registered with the Democratic Party (which he reiterates that he only did to help get Bernie Sanders elected), he vehemently states that he is an independent when it comes to politics. In his mind, everyone should get an "F" as a grade for their performance—the President, the Congress, and the Supreme Court—noting that "the government functions only to help corporations get rich and make money."

One of David's biggest turn-offs was what he called "those neoliberal corporate Democrat types," embodied by the Obamas, the Clintons, and the Bidens. He thinks that they are purposefully not addressing an issue that threatens to exterminate the entire species—climate change—as "the capitalist system is collapsing and, in its wake, destroying the entire planet."

David was particularly disappointed by what he saw at the DNC, making him dislike Clinton even more than he originally did during the primaries. "You talk about collusion—there was collusion at the DNC!" he asserts passionately. He recalls millennials who he knew spent thousands of dollars that they didn't have (because they were paying off student debt) to go to the DNC so that they could be part of the debate. "And what did the Democrats do to them? They put Hillary signs in front of these kids' Bernie signs. They cut off the lights in the sections where the Bernie people were. It was blatant corruption; they even gave Clinton the nomination before the vote because they were counting the corrupt superdelegates. Of course, the youth walked out in protest."

After the DNC, David resigned himself to the fact that Trump was most certainly going to win the election. He believed that there was no chance that Clinton could come back and gain the support of the progressives that she so desperately needed to win. "The Rust Belt Democrats who lost jobs because of her husband were specifically going out to vote against her; the millennials said 'screw the whole thing,' and there were a ton of Republicans who would come out just to vote against her, too," he comments. As the general election neared, David decided that he needed to focus less on party politics and more on issues that mattered deeply to him. He and his wife went back to their progressive roots—helping the homeless and thinking about how they could better help fight climate change. When the Dakota Access Pipeline protests gained traction, the two of them decided to hop over the pond to South Dakota to support the Lakota people at Standing Rock.

Just as the Sanders-Clinton contest divided the Party during the Hawaii State Convention, the divide was also obvious within the four chosen Hawaii electors. David claims that two electors were clearly Clinton supporters, while he and one other elector had originally shown their support for Bernie Sanders. Elsewhere in the country, Bernie supporters doubtlessly found themselves among the esteemed members of the

Electoral College, but David was such a huge Sanders supporter that some of his friends were clearly afraid that he might go rouge. He remembers when one of his good friends brought up the Electoral College vote out of the blue, commenting, "he told me that I had a responsibility to vote for Clinton; that I had signed some sort of pledge to vote for her."

As David thought back over the last few months, he swore he did not remember being asked to sign a pledge to vote for Hillary. Moreover, if asked, he was certain that he would not have agreed to it. "No one ever said, 'Raise your hand. As an elector do you solemnly swear to pledge your vote for the Democratic Party nominee?'" he asserts. "Perhaps one of the forms I filled out had something about a pledge, but no one ever mentioned it to me." He developed the belief that the forms were probably tools that the old guard Democrats were using to compel the electors into doing what their party said they must do.

Every time he thought about voting for Clinton, David couldn't see himself actually voting for her. These sentiments were confirmed when he stumbled upon a video on the internet contrasting Bernie's and Hillary's speeches during the state primaries. "In Bernie's speeches, he always focused on the 'we,'" David remembers. "Bernie said things like, 'We can make change happen' or 'We can build a better 'tomorrow.' Whenever Clinton spoke it was always about the 'I.' She said things like 'I want this' or 'I did that.'" In David's mind, there was a clear difference between the two candidates: Bernie wanted to accomplish things for the working people, while Hillary Clinton just wanted power.

He began to think seriously about what it would be like not to vote for Clinton. As he did more research on the internet, he realized that the Constitution gave all the electors the power to vote according to their personal choice. He was sure that he had been voted as an elector at the Hawaii Democratic Party convention by his fellow Berniecrats, not by

Clinton supporters. He wondered if his loyalty should be to this group who had voted him as elector, rather than to the entire party. Simultaneously, he knew that the local Democratic Party would be vehemently against his Bernie vote and that there could possibly be repercussions if he didn't vote for Clinton.

David clearly remembers the day of December 19, sitting down with the form in front of him and staring at it. He began thinking: Clinton had already lost; the house had already been burned down. Why pretend that he was a Clinton supporter, when he clearly wasn't (and never was)? "I began to think about the election process and about the millions of people who voted for Bernie because they believed in him," David remembers, with passion filling his voice. "Hillary Clinton had done nothing to earn my Electoral College vote. In fact, the Democratic nomination was stolen from us: from us Bernie supporters."

He knew that Hawaii had a secret ballot, so he decided to put down Sanders's name. He felt that in that moment, he had made the right decision. When the results were read out loud, David says it was like you "could hear a pin drop in the room. There was some chatter before, but now everything had just fallen into dead silence." He looked around and saw the reactions of some of the others; one "old guard" Democrat's face was so red with anger that David thought it was possible that she was having a fit.

Someone asked the Attorney General of Hawaii if the Bernie vote was valid. To David's relief, the Attorney General replied without hesitation that the Constitution stipulated that electors could vote according to their personal convictions and certified the vote for Bernie Sanders on the spot. As soon as the ceremony ended, commotion took over. David's fellow Berniecrat on the Electoral College had supposedly said that they were considering backing Sanders instead of Clinton. People came running over to the other elector looking for some type of explanation, but the elector looked so confused that people started second-guessing themselves. When the elector stammered that it wasn't their vote, David decided that it was time that he owned up to his Electoral College vote.

David recounts what happened next as a whirlwind beyond his control: "Suddenly, there was media all over me. There were cameras in my face." In the midst of the chaos, he clearly remembers the old guard Democrat running up to him and sticking her finger against his chest, threatening: "I am going to get you. I am going to bring you down." David knew that the threat was legitimate, but at the same time, he wasn't all that concerned. As she screamed at him, he couldn't help but smile as he thought about how the Hawaii Attorney General had just approved his vote. He had succeeded. Nothing—not even an "angry old vitriol-spitting Democrat"—could take this moment away from him.

As the media asked him question after question, David realized that he had been given a platform to share Bernie's message and make a stand for Bernie supporters across the country. Even now, he comments that he cannot believe that he was the only 2016 elector who was successfully able to vote for Bernie Sanders. When asked by the media if he was afraid of a potential fine or even a jail sentence for his vote, David claimed that he wasn't because "I did the right thing. When you know what the right thing to do is, you cannot worry about the potential consequences. You just have to do it."

Inwardly, he knew that he would never pay any fine that they might throw at him, and he was not afraid of going to jail. He thought about everything that he had been through in his life—all of the protests that he had participated in and organized. ("Thank goodness, tear gas was only used at one of the protests," he later commented to me.) He thought about all of the times that he had been thrown in jail overnight as a teenager

in California, held for 24 hours without being charged with any crime—
what he says was normal for long-haired teenagers and young people
who "didn't fit the mold" in the tumultuous 1960s.

"It was horrible back then because they were still doing strip searches,"
he recounts to me. "You would have to take off everything but your pants.
When you removed your shoes and socks, the road would be so cold under
your feet. We would be shivering there half-naked on the side of the road."
Once he was thrown into jail after talking back to a cop, when his car was
stopped and his date's purse was illegally searched to reveal that she had
unidentified pills. When it was determined that they were mere diet pills,
formal charges never materialized, but when relatives came to bail him
out, the police claimed that he had been moved to another jail and had
gotten lost somewhere in the system. That frightful night, David shared
a cell with a drunk man who terrified him, only to be released the next
morning and discover that his cellmate had murdered his entire family
the night before. There was no way that he could face anything worse
than that in a Hawaii jail after his Electoral College vote.

"People can certainly make the case that what I did was a simple protest vote," David claims. "Maybe it was. But the way I view it, I had one
opportunity to do the right thing." David truly believes that if Sanders
had won the Democratic nomination, he would have won in the general election against Trump without question. "But my Electoral College
vote doesn't necessarily belong to Bernie Sanders—it belongs to all of the
people who worked so hard to get him elected." Having spent more than
a year campaigning for Bernie, he had constantly been inspired by the
"millions of volunteers who had worked their asses off" to try to get him
the Democratic nomination. "Those people earned at least one electoral
vote, so I gave it to them," he exclaims.

David views himself as somebody who stands up for people when others won't. His Electoral College vote wasn't necessarily a responsibility, per se, but an opportunity for him to make people's voices heard. "According to my indigenous heritage, we are warriors. It is our responsibility to take care of people." He stipulates that his motivation was solely this—that he was not making a political statement or trying to get his name in lights. In fact, he laughs now at his lack of understanding of what being in the Electoral College meant at all. "I didn't realize until the day of the vote itself that my name and my vote were going to be in the Congressional Records."

He now describes voting for Bernie Sanders as an elector in the Electoral College as "among the proudest moments in [his] life." Sometimes he questions his entire participation in the Electoral College system, considering that he remains completely against it from a philosophical standpoint. He has tried to make peace with the juxtaposition; saying that he was just doing the job that other people asked him to do and that the Democrats who elected him were his friends and colleagues in the Sanders camp.

"When I voted for Bernie, I didn't think about the history books, I didn't think that it could become some national scandal," David comments. As he drove home, he began to wonder: what would people say? How would they react to his having voted for someone who didn't win Hawaii's popular vote? These thoughts flooded his mind when he checked the messages on his landline's answering machine and saw that it had crashed. Then, he turned on his computer and saw that his Facebook had crashed.

The story of his Electoral College vote made both local and international news. He began reading through some of the messages and was overwhelmed with emotion. There was no negativity—all of the comments that he saw were positive—thousands and thousands of people thanking him for what he did. "As soon as I saw that, I knew that I had done the right thing," David tells me, his voice still full of purpose. "The nomination had been stolen from Bernie; the election had been stolen. All I did was validate all of their efforts—all of our efforts—to make the world a better place. At that moment, I felt so proud. I thought to myself: This isn't my protest vote; this is our protest vote. This is our stand."

Bill Greene

Part 3

By the time the Electoral College vote had rolled around, Bill Greene was beyond frustrated, but at the same time, as a political scientist, he was fascinated. He had received over 90,000 emails, making him go over his school's allocated mailbox space on a daily basis. The Hamilton Electors and Daniel Brezenoff's Change.Org petition had empowered a new generation of internet activists, who desperately wanted Bill to change his Electoral College vote. It was near the end of the semester, which meant that his actual students' emails asking questions about exams and term papers kept bouncing back to them.

He wasn't surprised, however. As soon as the general election happened, he had a feeling that things might get really crazy, so he made most of his social media accounts private. The only contact information that people could find for him was his school address, where he even received about a dozen snail mail letters. He felt lucky because he was in a private Facebook group of Texas electors and was seeing the ordeal that they were having to go through. At first, they were just posting photos with a daily stack of letters. Then, all of the sudden, he began to see them posting photos with USPS bins and buckets full of letters.

The vast majority of the emails that Bill got came through online forms like MoveOn, so most of them were pre-written. When he did receive an email that was tailor-made for him, his political nature made him want to respond to all of them. Eventually, he gave up on that. He was also a bit disappointed in the arguments: "Basically, 90 percent of the emails said something like Clinton won the popular vote, so you need to vote for her. But then there was always a caveat, saying that if I didn't want to vote for Clinton to please not vote for Donald Trump." Bill was completely against the popular vote argument, so the emails fell on deaf ears, but he was still enthusiastic that so many people were learning about the Electoral College.

Bill realized that he was one of the lucky ones, because some of the other Texas electors were posting in their private Facebook group about threats of violence that they had received, saying that they and their families were in danger. These were immediately forwarded to the FBI to determine their validity. The only thing that Bill got in one of his letters was a threat that he didn't even view as a one: "You better vote the right way, or else."

As the election neared, Bill began to notice that the communication became more personalized and more high-level. Academics started to reach out to him, including Texas political science professors, as well as Harvard professor Lawrence Lessig. Lessig, who had run against both Clinton and Sanders early in the 2016 Democratic primary, was in the middle of a campaign called Electors Trust, in which he claimed that he would provide financial and legal support for any Republican electors willing to vote against Trump. Even in the days leading up to the election, it was reported that Lessig thought that he might still have been able to convince some 20 Republican electors to switch sides, a wave that groups like the Hamilton Electors hoped would embolden more electors to stand up and vote their conscience. Bill was enthusiastic to have the attention of these academics and corresponded with several of them.

He remembers, "Some people were calling the Hamilton Electors a conspiracy." (Indeed, Fox News had multiple headlines, providing the breaking news of how one celebrity or another shared their support for possible electors to go against Trump). But according to Bill, "it didn't feel like that at all. It felt like a Hail Mary attempt in the final seconds of the game. People suddenly realized that Trump was actually going to be their President, and they were trying to find any way to stop that from happening. Let's throw all of the spaghetti we can against the fridge and see what sticks. It smacked of desperation." At the same time, Bill claimed that he understood it; a lot of his friends were completely blindsided by Clinton's loss.

What none of the Hamilton Electors or activists knew, however, was that Bill had already made up his mind on his Electoral College vote. After receiving the electorship, he really got into the process of trying to understand how the writers of the Constitution intended the Electoral College to be run. He started digging through The Federalist Papers, James Madison's notes during the Constitutional Conventions, and pronouncements from the Founders. The more research he did, the more the Founders rose in his esteem as brilliant leaders. "They were well versed in history and politics," he gushes. "And they didn't always agree with each other, so they built a system based on compromises." After his research and some conversations with old friends from his years in Republican politics in

Georgia, Bill quickly made up his mind to vote his conscience for whom he believed to be the most qualified candidate.

There was no "aha" moment; Bill claims that it was the result of a long process of his thinking through his beliefs and his options. He thought through the history of the Electoral College and how it had developed over time. "I won't deny that how the Republican Party treated Ron Paul during the 2008 and 2012 election process definitely impacted how I viewed my obligations to the Republican Party and its traditional establishment," he admits.

In the week before the vote, Bill noticed an interesting trend: Republicans were getting antsy. He began to get calls, emails, voice messages, and text messages from Trump campaign officials, as well as local and state officials from the Republican Party. They were trying to do headcounts to make sure that they had enough electors for Trump's win. Texas had suddenly (and quite unexpectedly) become a battleground state. Art Sisneros had dropped out of his position, saying that based on his Christian principles, he couldn't bring himself to vote for Trump. Already, Texas officials knew that they were going to have to replace Art the day of the vote, a move that might come with risk. Additionally, Chris Suprun had allied himself with the Hamilton Electors after a stirring op-ed in the *New York Times* and a massive press conference.

Bill didn't respond to any of them. Firstly (and conveniently), he says that he was too busy with the end-of-the-semester happenings to worry about anything else. But at the same time, he was a bit irked by their insistence. "I don't give a flip about parties at all," he says passionately. "I have been active in the Republican Party not because I support the party blindly, but because I support certain principles, and the Republican Party has been the best mechanism to fight for those principles."

By the time that he and his wife went to Austin a few days before the Electoral College vote, Bill was one of the men of the hour: party leaders definitely wanted to confirm his loyalty before the big day. The weekend before the Monday vote, there were many social gatherings. Bill remembers that during one, he was cornered by the chair of the Texas Republicans, as well as some people from the Trump campaign. "They said that they had been trying to reach me and they wanted to make sure that I was going to do the right thing," Bill remembers, with a hint of rebelliousness even in his voice today.

"I replied that in the state of Texas, the vote is a secret ballot and that I hadn't even told my wife whom I was going to vote for just yet. I could tell that this was not the answer that they were looking for, so I added in one last phrase: 'I will definitely be doing the right thing tomorrow and Trump will definitely win the vote.'" After that, Bill just walked away.

On the day of the Electoral College vote, Bill's college had sent two vans of students to watch the vote. It was after final exams, school was already out, and there was no way that the kids could get extra credit or brownie points, so Bill was impressed. Many of them were students who Bill had in his classes and he was hoping that he was going to make the election a memorable one for them. But as he walked into the State House, he was a bit nervous: he saw what he estimated to be a couple of hundred people outside protesting. Even when they got inside the Chamber, Bill could still hear their chants.

The day was rife with chaos and insecurity, because the very red, Republican state of Texas had suddenly taken on newfound importance: with the second-largest number of electors, the state's votes would have to be counted before Trump could officially be declared the nationwide winner. Before anyone could vote, four electors had to be replaced, and the Texas Republican Party didn't want anything to go out of the ordinary for that.

The first elector who had to be replaced was Art Sisneros. "There were two people who worked for congressional offices in Texas and according to the law, someone who works for the federal government cannot be an elector," Bill starts schooling me in the middle of his interview. "Then Texas state law came into play: There was one guy who was running to be a county commissioner or something like that. He had to either resign his office to remain an elector or give up being in the Electoral College." Bill doesn't remember exactly whom they chose in their places, but he thinks that at least one of these individuals was replaced by their spouse. Another thing that Bill remembers is that the replacement process took hours upon hours. Donald Trump could not be elected President without Texas, which meant all eyes were suddenly on the Lone Star state.

When it was time to vote, Bill was given a piece of paper that had two boxes, one of which he had to check. The first box had Donald Trump's name beside it and the other box had a blank beside it. The Vice President's ballot looked the exact same. Bill knew what he had to do. He wrote down Ron Paul's name for President. He still voted for Mike Pence for Vice President. When he went up to submit his vote, he kept on repeating a quote in his head by John Quincy Adams that he had read while researching the Electoral College. Although Adams was commenting on what it means to have the ability to vote, Bill felt it all the more strongly because he knew that his vote truly counted: "Always vote for principle, though you may vote alone, and you may cherish the sweetest reflection that your vote is never lost."

When it came time to read out the results, many protestors had given up protesting and were sitting in the Gallery. The entire State House was teeming with Capitol police and Bill wondered what it might mean. As it was announced that Donald Trump had won, there was screaming and crying from the Gallery, extremely emotional outbursts, which Bill's students filmed, and which he later watched. When the defects were announced, Chris Suprun's vote was certainly no surprise: he had been extremely vocal. "But the vote for Ron Paul was certainly not anticipated," says Bill, who remembers a lot of grumbling from the other electors around him. "I think that my students who were sitting in the Gallery immediately knew it was me, though. Not because I was a Ron Paul supporter in the classroom, but because I had always reminded them in my classes that constitutionally, electors could always be free agents.

After a perfunctory photograph with other electors in front of the Christmas tree, Bill and his wife went on vacation. He knew that people were probably going to trace the Ron Paul vote back to him soon, and he wanted to avoid the spotlight as much as he could. After his vacation, he reopened all of his social media accounts and was pleasantly surprised by the lack of negative feedback. "Among the Liberty community and movement online, there were a lot of responses and messages waiting for me. Almost all of them were messages of appreciation, saying 'thank you,' or happy that Ron Paul had gotten an Electoral College vote because they really believed that he deserved it."

He knows that he pissed off a lot of Republican Party people. As his vote didn't change the outcome of the election, their frustration was tempered. "Even so," he told me, "a lot of Republicans have said that though they don't agree with what I did, they recognize that it was my right to do it. They believe in the Constitution and want to uphold it."

In spite of this, Texas legislators introduced bills in two different legislative sessions to bind the votes of faithless electors like Bill (whom he doesn't refer to as "faithless," but rather as "free agents.") He notes that after 2016, he thinks that although political parties will work much harder at binding the votes of faithless electors, it will be difficult to actually achieve that. Sometimes he wonders why there haven't been more faithless votes, "In 2012, there were a lot of Ron Paul delegates, and there was a strong push against Mitt Romney. I have heard rumors that two Texas electors were planning on voting for Paul regardless, but a lot of backroom negotiations somehow managed to change their minds."

Bill calls his faithless vote his "last hurrah for party politics," even though I kind of doubt it. Bill seems to get himself into a political situation wherever he goes. He reiterates to me a belief which he holds deeply: "You can support a party and be active in a party, and you still don't need to agree with everything the party does."

It seems like Bill has finally checked one more item off his bucket list. He is excited to think that his Electoral College vote might encourage others to think about the presidential election process. "Now when I teach about the Electoral College, it takes a day or two," Bill comments enthusiastically, telling me that he typically saves the best for last: he doesn't tell his students that he was an elector himself until the very end. "I normally end the section by showing the 2016 Electoral College map and I point to that one little block in Texas that says 'Ron Paul' and I tell everyone that it is me. Some of them seem really excited by this. All of a sudden, the Electoral College is not a foreign institution, a bunch of faceless people somewhere doing something. They can put a name and a face to it."

Bret Chiafalo
Part 3

Looking back on the chaotic month of December 2016, Bret Chiafalo jokes that he felt like a lot of what he did with the Hamilton Electors was just putting out fires. There was daily bureaucracy he had to deal with and daily setbacks they were facing. The 40 days were a blur of emails and conference calls, as well as mundane tasks like filling out the paperwork to get the Hamilton Electors their 527 status or setting up a bank account. Major money was pouring in, sometimes at a rate that was too fast for them to even deal with. At one point, $100,000 was stuck in PayPal, because the company required a document to release the funds that simply hadn't arrived yet.

Once money started coming in, Bret felt a major change in the Hamilton Electors: they actually had a shot at making a difference in the December 19 Electoral College vote. With Mr. D and the network of volunteers he brought in, Bret and Micheal found themselves in contact with Hillary Clinton and John Kasich's advisers. At one point, Bret was convinced that they also had a direct line of access to Mitt Romney, only to find himself later corrected. He discovered that politics was often murky, with contacts and ideas shared by proxies.

The nature of what the Hamilton Electors was discussing was extremely sensitive. Bret knows that they doubtlessly had a lot of overlap with other groups like Unite for America and Harvard University professor Lawrence Lessig's Electors Trust, but each organization wanted to retain the confidence and privacy of the Republican electors with whom they had been speaking. He knows that this meant that they likely didn't share information that would have been very helpful, but Bret believes that this was non-negotiable. "We wanted every elector, whether Democratic or Republican, to know that they had complete control over their participation and narrative," Bret noted, commenting that Washington Democratic elector Esther "Little Dove" John refrained from media appearances, even though she agreed to be a Hamilton Elector. "We knew it was a sacrifice; [Texas Republican elector] Suprun's family even had to go into hiding, for goodness sake."

Bret remembers hearing the number 50 being bounced around a lot, and as he begins to talk through the states and the electors that the Hamilton Electors had been in contact with, he truly believes that almost 50 electors were seriously thinking about not voting for Trump. He asks me to remove specific details about the electors from my writing, but comments that he believed that they had made inroads with Texas, Utah, Ohio, Wisconsin, and Michigan electors.

"We had more than 40 electors whom we knew for a fact disliked Trump so much that they were considering not voting for him. Some were terrified of him. They didn't say that they were actually going to do it, but they definitely expressed the possibility of doing it," Bret recalls. "The problem that we faced is that each elector wanted the assurances that the others were going to do what they said they were going to do. It was like a messed-up chicken-or-egg situation. They didn't realize that some things have to be done on faith and faith alone."

Unlike Micheal, who questioned the intentions of some of the pro-bono leadership that had come on board, Bret recognizes that a lot of things went wrong and a lot of decisions were made that he wouldn't have made himself. However, he stresses, "I believe that all of the high-level volunteers did the very best they could do with the resources and the time that we had available to get this movement up-and-running. It is what it is." In order for it to grow, he relinquished a lot of control. "There was no time to be part of every decision that was being made. Time, time, time: we simply just didn't have enough of it."

As the organization grew, so too did the number of voices within the organization, who believed that they knew what was right for the movement to grow. "One of the topics that started coming up every day was whether we should just pick a Republican candidate and announce that we were all going to back him as Hamilton Electors," Bret remembers. The problem was, he didn't know which candidate they should pick. Should they pick a Republican establishment guy like Mitt Romney, knowing that they could likely sway the Utah electors? (Donald Trump only won 45.5% of the popular vote of the traditionally Republican state; with Hillary Clinton getting 27.5% of the vote and Utah native Evan McMullin getting around 21% of the vote.) Or should they pick Ohio governor John Kasich, a popular moderate Republican, who might also sway some moderate Democrats, creating a truly bipartisan movement?

"I think that we were holding out for the idea that one of these candidates would just jump on board and fight alongside us," Bret comments.

When no one offered, the Hamilton Electors didn't pull the trigger and choose a candidate. Bret even remembers a high-level volunteer calling him up the day before the Electoral College vote, begging him just to come out and say that they were supporting Romney. "In hindsight, if I could do the whole thing over again, I would have definitely named a candidate," he muses.

In the midst of the Hamilton Electors gaining steam, Bret was starting to get scared. People were talking about civil unrest if Bret and Micheal were successful. "They were saying things like we were going to be overthrowing the will of the people and, as a public face of this movement, I knew that I would be in the line of fire." He started talking with a friend, who put him in touch with another friend, who developed a contingency escape plan that Bret would go to Denmark if the Hamilton Electors turned out successful. Bret also started shopping for bulletproof vests and comments that if he made more disposable income, he definitely would have bought one. "I thought to myself: who would be an easier target? Baca, the former marine? Or me, the tech nerd?" Bret comments, sharing details of a well-formed contingency plan that he never had to act upon.

The night before the historic Electoral College vote, Bret felt surprisingly calm. He knew that he had done everything he possibly could for the Hamilton Electors; there was nothing else that he could do at that point. Considering that when he first started this Hail Mary attempt to stop Trump from becoming President he thought that there would be no Republican electors joining in, the fact that they had gotten Chris Suprun already meant that they were successful. What Bret didn't know is whether they just were going to have only one Republican elector join them, or fifty.

Much earlier in the process, Bret had made peace with the fact that he was not going to vote for his progressive beliefs as an elector. Instead, he was going to follow the promise that he had given every single Republican elector with whom he had spoken: He was going to vote for a qualified Republican as President. Although I ask him what the process of rationalizing something like that was like, Bret throws off the question, responding that it was just something that he knew that he "had to do" in order to gain trust and maintain credibility with the Republican electors, whose support he was hoping for and counting on.

However, on the day of the Electoral College vote, as Bret made the three-hour drive to the State House in Olympia, it was clear from the East Coast results that things didn't go the Hamilton Electors' way. He had a lot of time to think about everything that had happened in the car, and became increasingly emotional. "I felt disappointed," he recalls. "I felt terrified for what was about to happen to the country. But at the same time, I also felt a lot of pride. I fought tooth and nail to try to impact and better the lives of millions, if not billions, of people across the globe. Yes, I had failed. But I knew that I had done something to be proud of." Having gotten an early start that morning, he arrived two hours early for the noon ceremony at the State House.

In spite of things not going his way, Bret didn't once consider changing his vote back to Clinton, or even to the candidate who had sparked his political engagement in the 2016 election cycle: Bernie Sanders. In the couple of minutes before they headed out to the floor, Bret turned to his two fellow Hamilton Electors in Washington state, Levi Guerra and Esther "Little Dove" John, and asked, "So, who are we going to vote for?"

When Levi Guerra responded that they should vote for General Colin Powell, Bret accepted her choice without any hesitation. When he asked about who they should vote for Vice President, Bret had one request: "I told them that I wanted to vote for a female Vice President because I didn't want to be hit as a misogynist by the Clinton people." Running out of time to discuss their options, they decided each of them would choose their own female Vice President.

Bret admits that he doesn't remember much else about the day, as he was running on pure adrenaline. He remembers seeing all of the protestors—people he recognized as their supporters, who had been showing up to one Hamilton Electors event after another—and feeling proud. He voted Colin Powell as President and Massachusetts Senator Elizabeth Warren as Vice President. He vaguely remembers making a speech to his supporters and doing a couple of interviews. On the long drive back home, he stopped over at a Popeye's and bought some fried chicken. When he got back home, he slept the best that he had in the last 40 days, since the general election results and the "moral electors" had been ideated.

"I crashed. I was emotionally, mentally, and physically exhausted," Bret remembers it taking him an entire year to spiritually recuperate and get to a better place. As he looks back on that time, he comments that the implications of what might happen if the Hamilton Electors succeeded or what might happen if they failed were extreme. For a long time afterward, he found it difficult to think past that succeed-or-fail dichotomy, describing himself like a bloodied and broken warrior.

Now years later, Bret sees a lot of good in his life having arisen from the Hamilton Electors. "I long struggled with self-esteem issues," he notes. "But when push came to shove, I got to show what I was made of. I stood up for what I believed was right, and it was extremely rewarding to fight for that. Doing something of this magnitude got rid of those little voices of doubt that were always ringing in my head."

Although he believes that he probably ended up doing 30–40% of the Hamilton Electors wrong, he says that there is very little that he would go back to redo, noting that it isn't healthy to always be thinking about what could have been, even though all of his fears about Trump have been realized in the last few years. "Federalist 68 said that electors needed to stop anyone who was unqualified, anyone who was a demagogue, anyone who was controlled by foreign powers. I did end up breaking my pledge to vote for Clinton, but in so doing, I believe that I was preserving the Constitution by trying to stop a clear and present danger from taking the White House."

Micheal Baca
Part 4

The day before the election, Micheal Baca thought there was a good chance that enough Republicans were going to go faithless, so as to throw the decision of who would succeed Barack Obama as President to the House of Representatives. Based on his work with the Hamilton Electors, he thought that there would be 14 to 19 people voting faithlessly on the day, seven or eight of whom he expected to be Republicans. They had reached out to two other groups that had been working on similar goals. One said that they had between three and seven Republican electors willing to defect, while another claimed to have 20.

Of course, the details were hazy. Many of these conversations were had not directly, but through intermediaries, who often talked in shadows. Everyone was extremely secretive about their numbers and contacts. Electors were becoming less and less willing to go public with their intentions the more the media campaign went on. "I was starting to get worried that in these numbers, we might be counting the same people twice, or even three times," Micheal comments. "But at the same time, I was optimistic. I had heard all along that there were other Republicans like Chris Suprun who were going to vote against Trump." Micheal was counting on the country's time differences to play a major role: once East Coast electors cast their faithless votes, they would inspire more electors in the Mountain and Pacific regions to likewise cast faithless votes.

Hundreds of protestors had gathered at the Colorado State House to support the faithless electors on the day of the election, after having participated in a candlelight vigil the night before. Not only had Micheal been vocal about his support for the Hamilton Electors, but other Colorado electors had also done the same. When the electors arrived at the State House to cast their votes, they were presented with a very specifically worded oath, which Micheal believes scared the other three electors who had also thought about voting faithlessly.

"Everyone was looking at me, and I felt really uncomfortable. But there I was, wearing this bright protest shirt, saying 'Enough is enough,'" Micheal remembers. When the Hamilton Electors lawyer told him to object to the oath, Micheal refused to sign. It was only when the Chief Justice came down from the Governor's office that he finally agreed to sign the oath. He signed it on the ground as a form of protest.

Even as he was voting, Micheal remembers thinking about what would happen if he still voted for Clinton. After all, it was clear that the nameless, faithless electors on the East Coast had not held up their side of the bargain. The thought crossed his mind that maybe he would still just vote for her because she was Hillary Clinton. Then the voting paper was handed over to him and it had only one name: Clinton. "Seeing that, I just couldn't vote for her," remembers Micheal. "So, I crossed out Hillary's name and I drew an arrow. And next to the arrow, I drew a square and checked it. Next to the square, I wrote out John Kasich's name."

What happened next, according to Micheal (and according to many constitutional scholars who have seen the legendary vote on YouTube) was completely unconstitutional. Micheal's vote was deemed invalid and chaos broke out at the State Capitol. "People were shouting out my name, screaming out, 'Let him vote.'" Micheal recalls. He himself also started shouting; words that he doesn't remember and that he now regrets. The moment was filled with emotion. Micheal was immediately replaced as an elector and was denied the opportunity to place a vote for Vice President. At the time, Micheal was scared about the consequences of his action. "I was afraid that they were going to take me away in handcuffs," he admits. "I didn't get put into prison that day, but I put myself into a different kind of prison through alcohol. I couldn't take it."

In our conversation, Micheal explains to me what should have happened from a legal perspective. It is clear that he is well-versed on the subject. After the vote, local Denver lawyer Mark Grueskin took on his case pro-bono, until it was clear that the state of Colorado would decline to press criminal charges. Then Harvard Law professor Lawrence Lessig picked up the case, which rose through the court system, with the Supreme Court eventually saying that they would issue a judgement on its constitutionality in 2020. "When electors are seated, they are acting on federal law, based on the Constitution," Micheal explains carefully. "Federal law is above state law and the Colorado state government should not have interfered with my vote in any way. Regardless, the ballot should have been counted before it had been read. It should have been signed, sealed, and sent to the U.S. Senate. If it was determined then that I had done something unconstitutional, it should have been at that stage, not before."

Micheal takes great pride in knowing that the case might make an impact on United States electors for years to come, calling the Hamilton Electors a Pandora's Box. "Someone who is more politically savvy than I am could potentially do something. I did not try to use the Electoral College for nefarious reasons, but someone could do that." In spite of quite a bit of negative attention, he is incredibly proud of his work with the Hamilton Electors, noting that 50,000 to 60,000 people showed up for their events and they got over 6,000 small donors. He thinks that it was a solid, bipartisan movement, although he had hoped that it might have been considered "post-partisan."

While Micheal has more or less recovered from his engagement in politics, the days and months following the election were extremely difficult for him. During Trump's inauguration, he returned to Washington, D.C. for a third time. This time, he went solely to protest. While there, he found himself disappointed with the man who brought him into politics in the first place: Bernie Sanders. When he saw that Sanders did not protest Trump's nomination on the floor of the Senate, he became increasingly angry at what he believes to be establishment politics. "No Democrat did anything in the Senate, including Sanders, because they were all just thinking about running for President in 2020," he comments, with a trace of sadness in his voice. "If people thought that Trump was so dangerous, why didn't they do anything about it?"

Throughout our conversations, Micheal constantly reminds me that he tried and failed to change the course of American politics, which inevitably leads him to the question of why others with more political power and knowledge didn't do something. "Every time I see Trump on the television screen, I cringe. When I listen to his speeches, I feel a lot of guilt and disappointment. In December 2016, 538 people had the opportunity to change the course of history. I wonder if I had done better, then maybe this wouldn't have happened. I tried literally everything that I could think of doing."

Claiming that this was the one chance for him to do something big in the world, Micheal tells me that he has thought non-stop for over three years about everything that went wrong and what he might have been able to do to make it right. "If I could have done it again, I would have done it differently," he tells me. "I would have created a campaign, complete with a political war room to recruit 37 patriots to go against Trump. I would have been strategic about what to say and how." Even as he says this, he questions whether this new strategy could even have worked. "I don't know what I should have done," he admits, "But I am constantly plagued by the phrase 'if only.'"

The Scholar
Part 2

Wh
en Robert Alexander of Ohio Northern University is asked about
his research, he tries to keep things simple. "Normally, I start from
the very beginning and remind people that when they go to vote in the
presidential election, they are not actually voting for the people on the
ballot. They are voting for people who will vote for President on their
behalf. If I am talking to a layperson, normally that is how far the conversation will go," Rob laughs. "They are blown away by this."

If the conversation does happen to continue and Rob begins to explain
his research on the characteristics of electors and the possibility of whether
electors might vote faithlessly, Rob finds that people start getting quite
upset. "A lot of people view our Founding Fathers as wise individuals and
they don't understand how the system could allow something like faithless electors. What they don't realize is how much the Electoral College

has changed—the institution that we have now isn't what the Founders originally set up," Rob comments, citing the Twelfth Amendment, which changed the very nature of the Electoral College.

Since his first elector survey in 2003, covering the 2000 presidential electors, Rob has given up his original research on interest groups to focus almost exclusively on the Electoral College. One of the things that clearly keeps him going is his own intellectual curiosity. "In a sense the Electoral College is such a narrow topic, until you start unpacking it and it becomes so much more. It is true that there are hardly ever faithless electors, but at the same time, it is also true that electors are thinking about voting faithlessly much more often than people expect. We go to bed the day after Election Night thinking and believing that we know how it is going to turn out. At the end of the day, we actually don't."

When I ask about the most surprising thing he learned through his research, he laughs and comments that it was the fact that electors were real people. Quickly, though, he expands on his answer: What surprised him the most was that the electors were contacted and lobbied by people who wanted them to change their vote. But what fascinated him even more was that some electors considered an alternative candidate after being contacted and lobbied. As the first person to research these electors, Rob has termed them the "wavering electors." Essentially, they might do what their party expects of them at the end of the day, but their compliance shouldn't necessarily be expected.

Ever since discovering that up to four of the Republican electors thought that George W. Bush had won the 2000 election illegitimately but still voted for him regardless, Rob has spent the last decade-and-a-half trying to figure out why some electors consider not conforming to their party's expectations. Through his surveys every four years, Rob has determined that the "wavering electors" are more likely to belong to a minority group than the average elector. Moreover, they are also less likely to have held public office in the past. "They are not as afraid of being marginalized, and perhaps are less deferential to the office. To them, rules don't matter as much," Rob conjectures. "They first consider their beliefs about what is right and wrong, rather than first thinking about politics." Citing studies that show that politicians act very differently during their tenure depending on whether or not they are up for reelection, Rob doesn't find this revelation necessarily surprising: it falls under what political scientists know about political behavior.

Despite his deep interest in the subject matter, Rob notes that his research has not always been smooth sailing; academically-speaking, the execution has been quite difficult. "When I wrote my first book that was finally published in 2012, there was no theory of electors. Creating a theory is hard work. Creating one that is actually publishable is even harder," Rob notes. Focusing his research on "wavering electors," he says the main theory of his first book was that a particular type of bombastic candidate could bring out wavering and faithless electors. "So, when the 2016 election came around, as a scholar, I just kind of wanted to laugh and say that I told you so," Rob notes, tongue-in-cheek.

Rob had a feeling that the 2016 election might be different when he attended the Republican National Convention in Cleveland as a spectator, noting that he felt that there was legitimate concern in the Republican Party's establishment about whether Trump's rise would bring instability to the party apparatus. At the same time, Rob wasn't counting on Republican defections; he had been through so many elections where he thought that electors might defect, just to have them all to behave themselves at the end of the day. Besides a 2004 incident in Minnesota (when an anonymous elector accidentally wrote down the Democratic vice presidential pick, North Carolina Senator John Edwards, for both President and Vice

President), nobody in recent elections had voted faithlessly, despite his research showing that many had considered the possibility.

In 2008, 90% of Democratic electors were asked to change their votes by conservatives who believed that President Barack Obama was not a United States citizen. Rob remembers 2008 as a potentially ripe time for defections. He had been at the Democratic National Convention in Denver, where he had overheard an Ohio delegate saying, "I am not going to vote for Obama. It's Clinton's turn." He was a bit surprised when, in spite of a contentious primary and a robust conservative letter-writing campaign against Obama, everyone came together and there were no faithless Democratic votes in 2008. He thought that the 2008 campaign might also result in faithless votes on the Republican side. Indeed, despite George W. Bush's two terms, no one from his administration rose as a nominee, leading to a rigorous primary that set up John McCain against strong Republicans like Mitt Romney, Mike Huckabee, Ron Paul, and Rudy Giuliani. Indeed, when Rob was going through the elector surveys, he was surprised to discover that some 20% of the Republican electors were potential "wavering electors." While it was unsure how much they actually considered the possibility of defecting, it had at least crossed their minds that they did not have to vote for John McCain in the Electoral College.

Of course, Rob knows that his data can be difficult to quantify. "It is hard to determine whether an elector is seriously considering defecting," he comments. "In the surveys, we give them a scale between 1 and 10. But what if someone writes down a 6? What does that really mean? I don't know. Maybe they thought about it, but they didn't strongly consider it. The scale is completely personal."

Again and again, our conversations go back to the deeply personal nature of the Electoral College, which makes it difficult to quantify and generalize from an academic perspective. Indeed, the Electoral College is not a monolithic organization, but a motley group of individuals with their own political priorities and beliefs. "Almost always strong Republicans and strong Democrats are chosen as electors. But say in 2016: being a strong Republican doesn't necessarily make you a Trump supporter. Nor does being a strong Democrat make you a Clinton supporter."

Indeed, while 538 electors every four years create a small sample size, the number makes it nearly impossible to track on a case-by-case basis, even if all electors were willing participants in such a study. As Rob and his students had discovered, it was hard enough to find all of the electors' addresses, let alone do more in-depth investigation into their backgrounds. That being said, their research was always full of surprises, like the time when one of the completed surveys was returned along with a Non-Disclosure Agreement because the elector was a reality television star. "So much about the Electoral College and faithless electors seems like it would belong in fiction, but the reality is actually crazier than what you can make up," Rob comments.

After both the Republican and Democratic Conventions in 2016, Rob had a feeling that the topic of the faithless electors might come out. Although he might have been surprised that Baoky Vu's piece came out so early, he didn't view it as that unusual in the grand scheme of things. He notes that there are typically a couple of electors in each election cycle who bring up the idea that they could vote for anyone for any reason. "Many electors see this as a way to make a stand for something, from abortion to taxation," Rob notes. Indeed, in 1988, West Virginia Democratic elector Margaret Leach became so upset that she could vote faithlessly from a legal perspective, that she ended up voting faithlessly as a protest, encouraging other electors to do the same (they didn't). What was different, however, in Rob's mind was how much both candidates seemed to be disliked within their respective parties. "In my 2012 research, I presented two reasons why there might be wavering electors. The first is that the electors don't like the candidate. The second is that electors are actually not that active in the party." It seemed like the situation was ripe for the first condition to substantially impact the election.

On Election Night of 2016, Rob was contacted by the CNN Opinion Editor, asking him to prepare a piece about the Electoral College. For Rob, it was a bit of an emotional experience. "For so long, I had been working so hard on trying to sell this idea to anyone who would listen. It was coming around once every four years," he remembers, describing the contact as a validation of his work. "All of a sudden, these people are reaching out to me."

Nor was it just the media reaching out to Rob. Within a couple of weeks, he was getting contacted by the nascent Hamilton Electors group. "When the Hamilton Electors sent me that email, everything just began to feel surreal," Rob remembers. "From an academic perspective, when are you given the opportunity to become a part of the research that you are doing? Most of our research just sits on a bookshelf somewhere." But Rob was adamant: he was not going to cross into advocacy. He wanted to maintain objectivity and credibility. When they asked for assistance in learning how to reach out to potential electors or learning how to target "wavering electors," Rob suggested that they read his book, trying his best not to sound rude. He was skeptical, not because he didn't find their mission fascinating, but rather, because a non-elector was contacting him on behalf of the Hamilton Electors. When the person suggested that they already had 20 to 30 Republicans considering defecting, Rob silently questioned the numbers in his head, chalking them up to wishful thinking.

One thing the Hamilton Electors certainly did, though, was to expand the knowledge of the Electoral College among the general population. As

Rob started to write a new book after the 2016 election, he was shocked to discover that the approval rating for the Electoral College was at an historical high in 2016. In his 2019 book, *Representation and the Electoral College*, he notes that according to the Pew Research Center, 44 percent of the population actually agreed with the Electoral College—up by nearly 10 percent, where it had stagnated in the mid-30 percent for decades. Perhaps it is due to the Electoral College being viewed as the "last line of defense" or a "break in case of emergency" against a potential threat to the presidency (the main idea that the Hamilton Electors put forth in their marketing campaigns) that its status increased so substantially.

If that is the case, it looks like public support for the concept of elector independence is on the rise, even though Rob notes that it is hard to find academics in the field who support the idea. He notes that the strict Constitutionalist Tara Ross, who has written a number of books in support of the Electoral College, has not fully backed elector independence, even though the Constitution doesn't say or suggest anything against it. Believing that it could become yet another reason why the general public could become increasingly cynical about United States politics, Rob believes that elector independence is an interesting topic because there is one group that seems to support it wholeheartedly: the electors themselves.

"The Twelfth Amendment was based on the assumption that electors would vote the party line and it took a lot more time and effort to agree upon than the original description of the Electoral College," he posits, "But electors like their independence. I guess they are thinking about other practicalities: What if a candidate dies? What if a candidate has a stroke? What if the candidate commits a crime? Would they still be required to vote for the candidate who won the state's popular vote in these cases?"

According to Rob's research, every Republican elector was lobbied in the 2016 election to switch their vote from Trump to another candidate, and at least one-fifth of the Republicans considered defecting. He was a bit disappointed but not surprised by the return of his mail-in surveys: while all his previous surveys had seen a return rate over 60%, this one fell to 50%. He knew that electors had been bombarded during the election, but he also heard that at least one other group was sending out surveys and questionnaires, which might have had an impact. (He has yet to see any published research with the data obtained from these other surveys and is ultimately unsure of which scholar or organization sent them out).

As he thinks back to the Hamilton Electors and the most unusual 2016 presidential election cycle, Rob comments, "Was it wishful thinking that 37 Republicans would have changed their Electoral College vote? Yes, it would have been completely unprecedented. Did 37 Republicans think about changing their votes? Yes, the data shows it. But did 37 Republicans seriously consider changing their vote? No, probably not." Remembering the comments written on the surveys, Rob notes that most electors feel a deep sense of honor and responsibility after being chosen for the Electoral College, and many of them equate that with the opportunity of representing the voters of their states. A lot of surveys said that while they did not agree with Trump personally, they could not pick their own personal conscience over the will of the voters they were supposed to represent. "You read Art Sisneros's blog posts about feeling torn about his electorship—those were absolutely heartbreaking," Rob comments, believing that other people likely felt similarly, even if they didn't make their struggle so public.

That being said, Rob doesn't exactly know what might have happened if East Coast electors had started defecting from Trump early on December 19. "Electors are rational," he mentions. "A 2004 elector wrote on his survey, 'I thought about it and I would have done it, if I thought it actually would have made a difference.' That was definitely also going on in 2016. People were thinking clearly about their options and making the calculations of whether they would vote faithlessly or not." Describing it akin to a dinner party where no one wants to be the first to leave, Rob hypothesizes how many electors it would have taken other than Chris Suprun to create a movement. "A herd would have followed eventually. Would it have been 37 electors? Maybe; probably not. Maybe if someone had been working behind-the-scenes to get a candidate like Pence elected, instead of Trump, it would have worked."

He knows that the electors were definitely concerned about their future in the party, noting Baoky Vu's decision to step down entirely. As we talk, we speculate if the way in which an elector was chosen actually might have an impact on whether or not they might go faithless. In his 2012 book, Rob had determined that political activity is correlated to how an elector was selected. In other words, if electors were selected at a convention, they were likely to be active in the party, whereas if a candidate was chosen by a party committee, they were likely less active than those chosen at a convention. Those chosen personally were most likely not active at all. "If they got chosen by a party committee, these electors are probably more sensitive about whether the Party Chair likes them or not, whereas the ones chosen at a convention might be more under the impression, 'I love my party, but I might not love my candidate,'" Rob hypothesizes. When I ask if narcissism could have played a role—that an elector wanted to put his or her name in the history books—Rob says that it is possible, but comments that while people may want to be famous, they don't want to become infamous.

As our conversation comes to an end, Rob comments that 2016 amazed him. Not only were there external forces pressuring electors, from Lady Gaga to a Saturday Night Live skit, but they were getting internal pressures from other electors. He recalls reading that there was a telegram movement to replace Kennedy as a candidate among the Democratic electors, saying that 2016 was like being able to see that up close. "When I think about it, I think that a lot of these electors had to have been extremely gutsy. Micheal Baca had a pre-printed ballot with only Clinton's name and wrote the name of another candidate instead. Levi Guerra faced a fine that she had no idea how she was going to pay. These are the types of people who don't conform to pressure."

Robert Satiacum
Part 3

On the drive to the State House to cast his Electoral College vote, Robert Satiacum was brooding. His wife, Elizabeth, sat next to him and was worried. She had no idea what her husband was going to do or what sorts of implications it might have. Admittedly, Robert didn't know what he was going to do either. By that point in time, he believed that politics was nothing but "a complete and utter joke." He was considering exposing the whole political system for the joke that it actually was, by writing down Water for President and Mother Nature for Vice President. But he also realized that would make him look a bit extreme, and he didn't really want to do something just for the sake of pissing people off.

But Robert had lost faith in the political system: a system that he claims put "Humpty Dumpty and Bozo the Clown up for election for President, and then forced everyone to choose what they viewed was the best

247

of two poisons." He suddenly began to feel affinities for the Jesse Jameses and Bonnie and Clydes of the world. "I think that in today's world, the pirates are probably the good guys," he comments soberly. He resolved that he was going to leave politics and political parties behind him.

But first he had to vote. Robert was constantly getting interview requests and wasn't sure what he should say, so he reached out to one of his friends who worked with him on conservation initiatives about two weeks before the vote. Robert claims that he was incredibly confused, and that he was considering voting for Clinton after all, just to make all of the controversies go away. The only thing that kept him from committing to that plan wholeheartedly was the fact that he had been written up so many times in cyberspace that he would never vote for Clinton.

"I don't know what I was waiting for," Robert remembers. "I think I was waiting for some golden lightning from the creator to light up the sky and tell me who to vote for." As he talked to his friend (a conversation that lasted less than five minutes), Robert began to feel more grounded. Not only did he realize that he didn't want to vote for Hillary, but also, he saw that the Electoral College was not a joke. "It felt like suddenly we had a nation that was full of Electoral College experts and they all had the answers to what I could do and what I should do. I seemed to be the only one in the entire country who seemed not to know what to do with my Electoral College vote."

Robert shunned the Hamilton Electors movement, even though he claims that Bret Chiafalo tried to reach out to him several times, wanting him to join. These interactions had an adverse effect: they made Robert feel even more isolated. He thought that the attention on all of the faithless electors kept his fateful interview from Standing Rock alive and well in the minds of the American public, whereas he just wished it would go away. "Besides," Robert comments, "why would I be all supportive of something about Hamilton and the Constitution? A lot of what the Founders said were lies anyway."

Robert's friend told him that he had to view his vote in the context of time—that people seven generations later would likely still be talking about it. He also told Robert that the entire country's attention would be focused on that person. Robert began to think deeply about what qualities made a good leader.

"Leaders make circles. They find the weakest person in the group and bring them into the circle of the community. The leaders give them acceptance and support because a good leader knows that they can only be as strong as the weakest link," Robert describes his ideas about strong political leadership, which are clearly influenced by his background. "The roots of leaders must be deep enough to keep them connected and grounded. They must feel a responsibility to the creator of all things." Robert also says that leaders must be coherent, compassionate, intellectually capable, and constantly thinking about the whole—not about what is wrong in the present day, but about how actions can affect children seven generations from now. As he thought about the leaders in the 2016 election, he knew that Clinton and Trump both came nowhere near his definition of a leader. Bernie Sanders was the closest thing that they had to a true leader in the election cycle. As they drove, Robert reminded himself of this yet again, and walked into Washington's State House with the intention to vote for Sanders.

This realization made him nervous, especially as he started engaging with some of the Democratic Party leadership. Although he wanted nothing more to do with politics, he still respected many people in the state party leadership. He knew that they wanted him to vote for Clinton, and at the end of the day, he really hated the idea of letting them down. He was very nervous, but when the ceremony itself began, he found himself with a sense of calm. It began with a flute song—Chief Dan George's song that Robert starts humming to me as he talks about it: *oh-weo-oh.* Robert began to think about his father out of nowhere. "The flute was singing to my heart; the water inside of my mind was slowing," he remembers.

When they finally sat down, Robert realized that things were getting real. He imagined hearing a drum roll: it was his moment of truth. "I was mad at myself at that moment. I was mad at my big, fat mouth that said that I was going to make this grand stand," Robert sighs. He kept his head down and says that he almost felt like he was back in grade school, finishing up a test that he didn't have the answers to, except that this test had only one question: his vote for President.

"I made my first line. I was just letting my hand do the job. The first line wasn't left to right; it wasn't diagonal; it went up and down." Robert just kept on thinking about what his friend had said: about this responsibility, which the next seven generations would talk about. In that nanosecond, in his heart of hearts, Robert felt like he knew what the country needed: "We needed an example of compassion and leadership. We needed a woman leader."

He looked back at the vertical line that he had just written; knowing full well that he was planning on making it into a "B" for Bernie. But Robert couldn't finish it. That "B" quickly became an "F" for Faith Spotted Eagle, the woman he had so respected that he brought his family to Standing Rock, to share his water vision with her. As soon as he wrote down Faith's name, he knew immediately who he wanted to be his choice for Vice President: environmentalist Winona LaDuke.

Robert was extremely proud of his choice. He knew that a lot of people who had supported Clinton did so because they respected her as a woman leader. He was proud to be able to provide another woman leader in her place. "I thought to myself: all of you want a woman leader? I will give you a leader who is a woman. And from her, you will get coherent truth. This is someone who has roots, who respects and accepts responsibility," Robert says. Faith Spotted Eagle was a woman who fit all of his characteristics of an ideal leader.

Robert knew that some people chuckled in disbelief when her name was first read out. "They didn't know what to make of it," he replied gracefully. (Indeed, the following month, then Speaker of the House Paul Ryan's smirk and eye roll was immortalized on C-SPAN tapes, when Robert's vote was read out during the formal congressional hearings on Inauguration Day.) Finally, Robert had made peace with his electorship, which he still claims came to him without him asking. He accepted responsibility, and with that, had cast the first two Electoral College votes that had ever gone to two Native Americans—votes that would indeed be discussed for the next seven generations to come.

Levi Guerra
Part 3

"It isn't surprising to me how little people actually know about the Electoral College," L.J. comments, somewhat soberly. "The reason I am not surprised is because I think about the amount of research that I had to do to just get the level of knowledge that I have right now about the Electoral College. And it wasn't just reading books; I actually researched by living through the process." Even now, she has a hard time believing that something as important as the Electoral College could be so misunderstood by the general public. When she mentions to her friends that she was an elector, they don't seem to understand its importance. "I don't think that my friends aren't smart," she kind of laughs, "But it shows that people don't seem to know what the real impact of the Electoral College is."

When the Hamilton Electors movement began to ramp up, she purposefully avoided the spotlight. Not only was L.J. nervous about speaking
in public, but also, she was extremely busy with work. Regardless, she
felt like much of her life between the general election in November and
the Electoral College vote was taken up by the Hamilton Electors. "It is
all kind of like a big blur to me now," she remembers. "I guess it is like
being on a teacup ride; everything is spinning all around you and you are
feeling nausea, mixed with a sense of uncertainty." Every time that she
got out in front of the cameras, she was extremely nervous about saying
something wrong, something that could mess up the entire movement.

One of her major contributions as a Hamilton Elector was sharing the
results of her summertime straw poll with Bret Chiafalo and Esther "Little
Dove" John. She explained that based on her constituency, she thought
that Colin Powell would be the best choice for President and that she was
planning on voting for him. Out of solidarity, the other two Washington
state Hamilton Electors agreed that they would also vote for him.

The details of the day of the Electoral College vote seem to slip L.J.'s
mind; perhaps because she was bombarded with so many things. Throughout our conversations, she apologizes that she doesn't remember small
details of the actual event, while she remembers other details extensively.
The day before the vote, she traveled to Vancouver, Washington to stay
with family. Many of the specifics escape her, but she remembers the night
before with family being refreshingly apolitical, without discussions of
the Electoral College coming up even once.

When she went to Olympia the next morning, it was raining. She was
surprised when she walked into the room and everybody already seemed
to know who she was. She was used to being kind of invisible. She knew
that her speech on the steps of the Capitol had made waves, but not that

nearly everyone in the room had already formed an opinion about her. "Nobody knew who I was before then. I was used to walking into a room and sitting down and maybe starting to chitchat with a few people," she explains. "This was something different. Everyone had already decided whether or not they liked me. And none of them had even met me." This type of attention was new for L.J., who was also surprised by the politeness and the civility with which one elector treated her, despite having written an op-ed that she needed to be jailed if she didn't vote for Clinton.

It was a new experience for L.J., as were many of the things that she encountered that day. "Looking around, I was in awe of how beautiful the building was," she remembers, "And I remember being completely in awe of the politicians that I saw in the building, walking about. I never before had met public figures in person. I just felt so small being there." Indeed, she later described the experience as akin to the field trips that she used to take in elementary school.

L.J. purposefully avoided the media, politely telling all of them "no, thank you" as she passed by. She was acutely aware that she didn't want to say anything stupid, which she would regret later in life. Additionally, she felt like the media didn't quite understand why she was supporting the Hamilton Electors to begin with: it wasn't her goal to not have Donald Trump elected President. All she wanted was to accurately represent her constituency through her presidential choice, as well as encourage the general public to think about the questions that had been bothering her about the Electoral College ever since she had been selected as an elector months before.

She remembers being intensely nervous. She doesn't remember details of the protestors or what they were saying; but rather the feeling of a lot of negative energy, crowding, and chaos. Ever the pessimist and preparing herself for the worst, she imagined what might happen if those people lost their tempers and considered bringing guns.

Unlike some of the other electors, L.J. describes no second-guessing on the day of the Electoral College vote. Since deciding upon Colin Powell, she never once considered changing her mind, although she hadn't come out and said publicly that she was going to specifically support him. She knew in her heart and mind that he was the best choice for her constituents, even if she herself was supposed to vote for Clinton. That sentiment was solidified when she made her public statement in support of the Hamilton Electors on the steps of the State Capitol. "I guess, if I said that I was going to do it and I didn't end up doing it, that would make me a liar," L.J. reasoned. "And I don't want to be a liar." She wrote down Colin Powell's name with no hesitation whatsoever.

When she was asked about her pick for Vice President, L.J. froze in utter panic. In all of her efforts to pick the perfect President, she realized that she had not done the necessary prep work to pick the perfect Vice President. "This just goes to show that I had zero clue of what the process was going to look like," L.J. comments. "There is no guide anywhere in the United States that shares with you how to be an elector; most people (myself included) just have to go with the flow."

A bit embarrassed that she had not prepared more for her choice for Vice President, L.J. began to rack her brain for who she thought would be a good pick. The first name that popped into her head was Massachusetts Senator Elizabeth Warren, but she wasn't sure if her local community would agree with that choice. L.J. remembers that she "decided to support one of Washington state's local political figures; someone that the people know, trust, and had voted into office before." She began to pore over all of the names of the senators and representatives from the state of Washington, when Senator Maria Cantwell's name popped into her head. Although she now believes that she probably would have picked a different candidate if given the opportunity to prepare more beforehand, she stands behind her made-on-the-spot decision. "I picked a candidate who my constituency had already chosen to represent them, so I think that they would agree."

When I asked her what Maria Cantwell's reaction was, L.J. chuckled, saying that she actually had no idea. She never had the opportunity to meet Cantwell before voting for her. "Now that I think about it, I wonder if she even cares," L.J. says, almost whimsically. "Who knows? Maybe she is pissed at me, wondering why I brought her into all of this."

Although she knows that it was an extremely important day with long-lasting implications, L.J. is quick not to make it into a saga. "That day, we walked into a room. We signed a piece of paper saying that we were electors. And then we made a choice," she summarizes. "That is what it is at its core. Life is simple like that."

By then, she was aware that her choices came with consequences, but she felt prepared to face the consequences head-on. She knew that she was going to be hit with a $1,000 fine, but now she had a team of lawyers and advocates who were willing to fight alongside her to bring it into the court system. Indeed, a short amount of time after she returned home, she received the $1,000 fine through USPS in a certified letter that she had to sign for. One thing that did surprise her, though, was getting a check to reimburse her for the estimated cost of her travel to the State House to vote as an elector. For L.J., it was a nice surprise, something that meant a lot to her, because it meant that electors didn't have to be and weren't expected to be wealthy. The state government had calculated the mileage between her home and the State House. She looked at the check, but she couldn't bring herself to cash it. It had been an honor for her to have been an elector. When she didn't cash the check, another check arrived; and when she didn't cash that one either, another. Eventually, they gave up.

Even though she talks nonchalantly about the day of the Electoral College vote, she comments that from the outside looking in, what happened that day was a really big deal. In another reality, she supposed that the Hamilton Electors could have convinced 37 Republicans to switch and block Trump's win.

In spite of the enormity of what the Electoral College represented, L.J. just decided to go on with her life. She kept working her way through school and even picked up an internship with an Oregon state senator. After focusing so much on national politics for so long, she was relieved to get back into what inspired her to get involved in the first place: local politics. "I think that local politics is so much more fulfilling, having that face-to-face interaction," she explains. "I liked to see how the state senator worked, sitting down and talking to constituents on a daily basis. I think that a lot of local policies are up-to-date with what the needs are, because people are hashing out these details, talking over complex subjects from housing to healthcare."

Despite her positive experience working for the state senator, L.J. still decided to pursue a career in the military. Although she had moved on, she found that the legacy of her Electoral College vote kept following her. "After bootcamp, I got a call from Bret Chiafalo, keeping me up-to-date on where we were from a legal perspective. And our court case kept on going from one level to another in the appeals process," she comments on how the Supreme Court had agreed to hear the Hamilton Electors case. "The news of the Electoral College never went away; it kept on popping back into my life."

Now, as she looks back, L.J. says that when the Supreme Court hears the case, it will actually be a bittersweet moment for her. "I have grown so much as a person over the last four years," she reflects, saying that she is heading to a U.S. military base overseas soon. "I started this journey when I was eighteen years old. And I will be twenty-three years old when it ends. The Electoral College has been an integral part of my story into adulthood and has helped me grow into the person I am today."

Epilogue

I was twenty-five years old when I stumbled upon the topic of faithless electors. I was in the middle of writing my master's thesis at Peking University in Beijing, China, in which I was analyzing the economic and trade relationship between China and the swing states of the United States presidential election cycle. As I sat with my thesis adviser, Wang Yong, he commented that I needed to include a chapter defining what a swing state was. To me, as a bit of a political nerd, it was a self-evident concept: how would I describe something that I found so intuitive?

As I sought to define a swing state, I found myself steeped in research about the Electoral College. Sitting in my small basement apartment, surrounded by stacks of papers and books about trade politics, I read one single sentence about faithless electors in an article and I was immediately intrigued. I cut myself some apple slices, sat down at my computer, and began to Google the names of the faithless electors. As I read about them, I found myself more and more captivated. Who were these people who were willing to completely alienate themselves from their respective political parties? What sorts of people would risk it all to do something that seemed so futile? What message were they trying to convey?

The hours passed, and, before I knew it, I had spent an entire day that was supposed to be spent writing my thesis stalking the faithless electors on social media. I spent the entirety of the next day reading about them. I later discovered that it was not thesis procrastination that made me so interested in the faithless electors; over the following months, these individuals kept popping up into mind anytime I heard or read something regarding the 2016 election. As Russian interference became a major talking point in the United States news media, I couldn't help but picture what a boon the Electoral College could prove to be for a foreign bad faith actor.

On and off for two years, I tried to get in contact with all the faithless electors I could, eventually interviewing many of them via phone and social media video calls. Despite my efforts, there are several who I could not reach and whose stories are not included in this book. Christopher Suprun is one of them. A former 9/11 first responder, Suprun was the only Republican elector to come out in favor of the Hamilton Electors. With his thirty seconds of fame also came infamy—his professional credentials were dragged through the mud and rumors were spread about his personal life. On the day of the Electoral College vote, he voted John Kasich for President and businesswoman Carly Fiorina as Vice President. Chris has since become a Democrat and remains active in Texas politics.

Esther "Little Dove" John is another Hamilton Elector. A Quaker of African American and Native American descent, Esther has been described by all who know her as an extremely kind and humble person, never seeking attention for herself, even though she is a Harvard-trained psychologist. Like Bret Chiafalo and Levi Guerra, Esther voted for Colin Powell for President. She also picked a moderate Republican for Vice President: Maine Senator Susan Collins. She found her name in the news in 2017, but not by choice: When she was kicked out of her Beacon Hill Seattle home in 2017 to make way for a new (and expensive) residential complex, the surrounding community was outraged and started a very vocal anti-gentrification project in her honor.

There were two additional faithless votes on December 19 that were invalidated. After voting for Bernie Sanders, David Bright, a raspberry and blackberry farmer from Dixmont, Maine, was asked by state officials if he would reconsider his vote. He said that he would vote for Clinton for President if he was given an opportunity to speak. He ended up giving a poignant and inspirational speech meant to encourage young Democrats, which can still be viewed on YouTube. Minnesota Democratic elector Muhammad Abdurraham also attempted to vote for Bernie Sanders as President and Democratic Hawaii Congresswoman Tulsi Gabbard as Vice President. Holding a PhD in Linguistics from the University of Minnesota in Twin Cities with study abroad experience in Taiwan, Russia, and Germany, Muhammad is now a start-up technology entrepreneur. He was removed as an elector in a very dramatic fashion during the ceremony itself. Additionally, Colorado electors Polly Baca (no relation to Micheal Baca) and Robert Nemanich later filed suits against Colorado, saying that they were planning on voting faithlessly alongside Micheal, but felt coerced into voting for Hillary Clinton on the day of the vote itself.

So often in politics, we see these picture-perfect individuals with their gorgeous families, with their perfect jobs and educational credentials. Looking at these polished and eloquent individuals on our news shows, it can be difficult to imagine a place in politics where normal, everyday people can actually belong and make a difference. However, as I wrote this book, I found myself time and time again touched by these imperfect individuals who were our 2016 presidential electors. As they opened themselves up and shared their life stories with me, I felt blessed in a way, even if that feeling was tinged with an overwhelming sense of responsibility to make their time, effort, and energy worth it. As I talked with them, laughing at funny stories of the Electoral College or simply listening as they shared their fears and insecurities, I thought about how the American political system allows a space for everybody to participate and their voice to be heard, regardless of their political background, job, or how much money they make. Having spent the last few years of my life in China, these conversations reaffirmed my faith in the American political system, by truly allowing a place for everyone.

At the same time, as I stepped back, I found the electors' stories extremely problematic when I considered the future of American democratic principles. How is it that 538 people, mostly nameless individuals who are known to practically no one, singlehandedly determine the leader of the free world? Never before had I questioned the Constitution as much as I did over the last year. I remembered back to when I was seven years old, when my parents returned home to South Carolina from an anniversary trip to Washington, D.C. and gave me a replica of the Constitution. As I gingerly unrolled the crinkled, seemingly ancient copy, filled with cursive scribbles that I was yet to understand, they told me that it was extremely important as the law of our land. Its contents seemed so sacred as not to be questioned. Indeed, I never truly questioned the Constitution throughout my childhood and young adult years—that is, until I grappled with what is the reality of the Electoral College.

In this process, I have personally come to question the term "faithless electors." This is the product of a great deal of thought as I considered what the word "faithful" truly meant, taking into account my personal experiences, my religious convictions, and my being a newlywed. If these people were truly faithless, I began to wonder to whom they had actually been faithless. One after another, these individuals confirmed and reconfirmed their commitment to their country, to the Constitution, and to their fellow Americans. They are certainly flawed individuals, as I believe that any one of them would readily admit, but they fought for a greater cause in the 2016 presidential election. I would venture to say that the only groups that these people have wronged or been unfaithful to are their respective political parties.

And yet, when these individuals describe their political journeys, I cannot help but think that perhaps these political parties have somehow not been faithful to them—that party leadership had priorities other than that of creating a dynamic environment that was capable of changing with the times, where people of differing political beliefs could find acceptance and understanding under a party platform, even if they don't entirely agree with all the others in their party. It may very well be that if political parties do not become more receptive to their constituents, the 2016 faithless electors may simply be a harbinger of what is to come. Future electors, as everyday individuals, may see their constitutionally-appointed responsibilities as doing what they believe is best for their constituents, rather than what is best for their parties.

There are several topics that I have just lightly introduced or not covered in this book, which I believe deserve more attention and research by other scholars and journalists. These include the stories of the Republican electors who considered defecting silently, but ultimately voted for Trump. Although this book is about the ones who made a public stand to vote faithlessly, standing one's ground privately is also making a stand. These electors' decisions should likewise be respected; they are the ones who decided that the stability and preservation of the system—no matter how flawed it might be—was better than an uncertain future. In addition, I couldn't help but notice that there were no conservative female voices that arose out of this narrative, which, due to my southern upbringing, I feel ultimately makes this narrative incomplete.

Additionally, I am concerned by two findings: first, that people from minority backgrounds are more likely to vote faithlessly, and second, that electors chosen directly by a state party committee, rather than by a state party election, are more malleable to party leadership and less likely to vote faithlessly. Based on the 2016 election, both of these rules seem to be true. However, I strongly believe that making it more difficult for people of diverse backgrounds to become electors would be detrimental to our government system, as would be removing the democratic component of the selection of electors. As state parties will likely try to consolidate their power over their electors, I hope that these do not become trends.

As I conclude this work, I feel compelled to share my personal opinion that the Electoral College should not exist in its current form, in which the general public doesn't understand the process by which their electors are chosen or why. The Electoral College should not be obscured by nebulous state laws and obtuse state party regulations. If it is to exist, we must bring this institution that our Founding Fathers created for us into the light, instead of allowing its flaws to fester in the shadows. Without a partisan agenda, we must talk about it, demand transparency from its governing bodies, and insist on its reform.

Postscript
After the Supreme Court

"So, what's new after the Supreme Court case?" Bret Chiafalo laughs. "Well, I recently got a snail mail notice from the office of Washington's Secretary of State that I am going to have to pay that $1,000 fine after all." For a while, he wondered if he would face the consequences of his faithless vote in the 2016 Electoral College or if the resulting fine would be lost to the memory of time. "My lawyers are reaching out for it to be reduced," he comments. "Maybe they will knock it down to one hundred bucks or something. They do that for speeding tickets all of the time."

Considering that the last four years of his life were building up for *Chiafalo v. Washington* to be argued at the Supreme Court to determine the constitutionality of state laws that bind electors, the result may have been slightly anti-climactic. Instead of witnessing the arguments live at the Supreme Court Building on One First Street NW in Washington D.C., he was relegated to listening to the arguments on his home computer in Washington state.

2020 proved to be an historic year for the Supreme Court due to the COVID-19 pandemic. *Chiafalo v. Washington* and *Colorado v. Baca* were originally planned to be among the group of arguments heard in late March. However, as coronavirus cases continued to rise in the United States, many were concerned about the health and safety of the justices, who were among the demographic most at-risk for infection. Six of the nine justices were over the age of 65; among which Ruth Bader Ginsburg was 87 years of age and Justice Stephen Breyer was 81 years of age.

When the cases were first postponed in mid-March, everyone was in the dark. Several of the electors commented to me that they wondered if the Supreme Court would leave them hanging. Speculations abounded that the arguments might be postponed until the next gathering of the Supreme Court and that the faithless elector cases would remain unresolved going into what was bound to be an eventful 2020 election cycle. There were sighs of relief when the Court announced that they would hear arguments via telephone conference, allowing the justices to work from the safety of their own homes.

The court also made the unprecedented decision to allow the proceedings to be broadcast live on CSPAN, giving normal Americans the opportunity for the first time in history to hear their justices in action. Although the broadcasting of Supreme Court cases is supported by the general public (some surveys show that upwards of 70 percent of the population support it), the Supreme Court has purposefully avoided doing so in the past. As noted by David G. Savage for *Los Angeles Times*, the Court was concerned that broadcasting cases could become sensationalistic, with lawyers playing up to cameras.

On May 13, 2020, Harvard Law School professor Lawrence Lessig (who founded the Electors Trust movement in 2016 to support Republican electors looking to defect from Trump) argued for the Washington electors in *Chiafalo v. Washington*. Jason Harrow, the chief consul for Equal Citizens (another organization founded by Lessig) argued for the Colorado electors in *Colorado v. Baca*.

"It was clear from the beginning what the justices were thinking," remembers author James McCrone, who tuned in to hear the arguments and discussed it real-time on Twitter with fellow Electoral College scholars and enthusiasts. "They just kept on using the word 'chaos' over and over again." Usually quiet in Supreme Court cases, Justice Clarence Thomas underscored how chaotic the system could become when he mentioned fictional *The Lord of the Rings* character Frodo Baggins in one of his questions:

> *Justice Thomas: The elector, who had promised to vote for the winning candidate, could suddenly say, you know, I'm going to vote for Frodo Baggins, and that's—I really like Frodo Baggins. And you're saying, under your system, you can't do anything about that.*
>
> *Mr. Harrow: Your Honor, I—I think there is something to be done because that would be the vote for a non-person, you know, no—no matter how big a fan many people are of Frodo Baggins.*

"They were not even considering our legal arguments," Bret remembers, "and they were taking our opponents' arguments at face value." Hearing the case argued at the Supreme Court felt like a win in and of itself for Bret, who relished in the conversations the case was sparking online. After listening to the justices, he certainly was not expecting a victory, but he was shocked when the decision was released on July 6: the faithless electors lost 9–0 in a unanimous ruling.

While media outlets across the country touted that the problem of faithless electors had been solved, those in the know couldn't help but to notice that the Supreme Court decision left gaping holes unaddressed. "The justices wanted to avoid chaos, but this might just be chaos forestalled," James comments, noting that all the Supreme Court said was that state laws to bind the electors are not unconstitutional.

"People think that the system is fixed—it isn't," says scholar Robert Alexander. "The Supreme Court essentially punted this issue down the field. They didn't want to tackle any more issues with this case than they absolutely had to. So, for most states, this doesn't really change anything." He notes that only 32 states currently have binding laws on electors, of which many of those are simply fines. Indeed, at the time of writing, only 15 states have the legal apparatus to remove and replace an elector after a faithless vote.

When asked if it is possible that state governments might adopt binding laws before the November 2020 election, Robert Alexander is skeptical. The issue is vastly misunderstood by the general public and there is not really the political capital to push them through. Practically speaking, most state legislatures are already out of session and will not reconvene until after 2021. However, perhaps the most complicated part of binding elector laws is that different state governments may have different interpretations about the constitutional role of electors. "The Texas legislature chose not to put a binding law on the books, even after the state had two faithless electors in 2016," Robert comments.

After the chaotic 2016 Electoral College vote in Texas, Texas governor Greg Abbott tweeted, "This charade is over. A bill is already filed to make these commitments binding. I look forward to signing it and ending this circus." In spite of the enthusiasm of the state's Republican leadership, there was never enough momentum to pass a bill through the legislative branch.

Perhaps Texas political science professor and faithless elector Bill Greene is to thank for the demise of the legislation. Bill passed away on July 3, 2019, at the age of fifty-four, but not before he made a stand against four separate bills to bind electors by giving four separate testimonies at the Texas House of Representatives in 2017. Commenting that he was surprised that the legislation was being proposed by Republicans who claimed that they were constitutionalists, he gave impassioned statements on the constitutionality of binding electors:

> I can say, without hesitation, that these bills—this one and the other ones that are being presented today—are prima facie unconstitutional. The Electoral College is one of the few remaining vestiges of the federal republican form of government that our Founders set up in the U.S. Constitution, and it's the Constitution that we should be most concerned with, and not knee-jerk reactions to the events of the day. Those authors of that document were quite clear that electors are to be free agents, capable of choosing whomever they believe to be the best qualified person in the country to be our chief executive officer. If you want to statutorily bind presidential electors, you might as well statutorily bind members of the Texas House of Representatives while you're at it. When the people vote YOU in, they have no control at that point, constitutionally, over your vote.

"States are completely in control of the Electoral College now," Bret comments. While Robert Alexander agrees that the Supreme Court's decision puts more power into the hands of state governments, he notes that it is not really out of the norm and that different states have different laws on a number of vital electoral processes—from mail-in voting to voting absentee.

For Bret, however, he is concerned that the Supreme Court ruling might make an "already unequal" Electoral College even more unequal than it was before. "You think about it: In some states, electors are completely free agents by law. And maybe in the state right next door, if an elector votes faithlessly, he or she will be thrown in jail. We answered one question of the Electoral College. There are still a lot that need answering."

Micheal Baca believes that many of the questions that his case presented were disregarded. On the day the Supreme Court released its decision, Micheal Baca called me on his way back from the gym. "I just got the news and my initial reaction is that the two cases got lumped together, even though they were very different," he stipulates.

"In Washington State, the state government at least allowed the ballot to be cast. They chose to fine them," Micheal comments. "In my case, all I did was violate a pledge and they removed me without allowing my vote to be cast. Was what the Colorado government did against the Constitution? Should my vote have been counted?" Micheal believes that the Supreme Court took an easier path instead of buckling down to answer these tough questions.

As for Robert Satiacum, he says that he fought the Washington state fine for his faithless vote tooth and nail, even if he didn't join the Hamilton Electors' court case. Stating that he didn't believe that he should be criminalized for his vote, Robert showed up three times to the local court to fight the fine. "Before each court date, the state sent me a huge stack of paper filled with this lawsuit," he remembers. "I just kept showing up and said that I would never pay that fine; that I didn't do anything wrong."

By the third time, Robert Satiacum was incredibly frustrated. He felt like his time was valuable and he was exhausted of wasting his days going to court. "I told the man in the black robes and all of those men in suits that they were just wasting their time," Robert remembers impassionedly. "They were wasting my time; they were wasting paper; and they were wasting so, so much money." He left and he claims that he never heard anything afterwards about an outstanding fine. "They have bigger fish to fry than faithless electors," he notes; although he is afraid that increased scrutiny with the Supreme Court case will make the fine magically reappear in his life.

Although the Supreme Court left many questions unaddressed, there is one question that continues to rise to the fore in the case of the faithless electors: Should the Electoral College even exist? To some, electoral independence is intrinsically linked to the role of the Electoral College itself. As Bill Greene argued in a separate testimony in the Texas State House of Representatives in 2017:

> . . . electoral "binding" bills are really just one more step in the elimination of the Electoral College. If you are going to bind the electors themselves in the Electoral College, then why have an Electoral College at all? Why have people elected by the people of Texas on November 8th of 2016, and then getting together on December 19th to cast a vote? Why do that at all? If it's really just a "ceremonial" thing, and it's just so that we can get together and have a nice dinner, then just eliminate the Electoral College. Go ahead and pass a constitutional amendment and get rid of the thing, and just go to a popular vote. If what we're interested in is, "Well the electors are supposed to vote according to the popular vote," whether it's in the state, or whether it's in the entire United States, then get rid of the Electoral College.

Many—both conservatives and liberals—are likely to agree with Bill's assessment of the importance of binding elector laws. Both Bret and Micheal say that the Supreme Court decision is likely to provide a bit of a legal boost to the National Popular Vote Interstate Compact (an agreement among states to award all of their Electoral College votes to whomever wins the nationwide popular vote) and hope to volunteer their time to that effort in the future. Bill's fellow Texan and Ron Paul supporter, Art Sisneros, thought similarly and was dismayed by the Supreme Court's decision. On July 9, he issued the following statement:

> I've considered the implications of the recent SCOTUS decision regarding the legal binding of electors. I was disappointed in the outcome of the case, but in no way surprised. Their decision was reflective of our culture at large. My experience in the Electoral College made clear that our nation desires a democracy. The understanding and principles of a republic are absent in the mind of the people. We get the government we desire, whether for our benefit or to our detriment. I believe in this case it is the latter. This decision simply moved the legal structure closer to the heart of the people. That is where our biggest problems lie, within us.

While it is certainly easy to draw partisan lines and say that faithless electors or binding elector laws have the opportunity to benefit one party over another, Baoky Vu comments that the very nature of politics is that it is quick to change. "Who knows? Maybe one day it will be the Republican Party that will be in favor of the National Popular Vote—and the Democratic Party will be against it," he comments. Regardless, he is personally in favor of the Supreme Court's decision, stating his belief that "someone has to play referee in all of this."

Baoky believes that the Supreme Court has actually remained as balanced as it possibly could be in this particular case. "All the Supreme Court did was rule in favor of state laws," he comments. "The Supreme Court didn't say that it had to be a certain way nationwide. They also didn't say that a state had to legislate on faithless votes. But the Supreme Court did give guidelines to legislate if a state wants to."

When I mention that Georgia has no laws binding electors, Baoky immediately knows where I am taking the question: Would he have felt empowered to vote faithlessly, if he knew such a stand was constitutional? He takes a moment to respond, saying, "Yes, this decision does reinforce that if a state has no such law, an elector is indeed a free agent." He insinuates that he still would have stepped down from his electoral post rather than vote faithlessly, due to his respect for his peers in the Republican Party.

Another reason why faithless electors cannot be relegated into the omnipresent liberal versus conservative debate is that the 2016 faithless electors exposed an additional division in the political system on both sides: the party elite versus the rank and file party supporters. In a statement provided on July 22, David Mulinix shared his opinions on the Supreme Court decision, as well as reiterated his belief that through his faithless vote, he actually followed the will of Hawaii voters:

> *Regarding the SCOTUS decision on the Electoral College, I am in agreement with their decision that electors must follow the will of the voters. More importantly than that, I am opposed to even having an Electoral College.*
>
> *This most recent Supreme Court decision is binding the electors to voting the will of the people. In a way, this makes the Electoral College unnecessary—which is nearly as good as getting rid of it altogether. When I was an elector in 2016, we could have overruled the will of the*

voters and put in who we wanted. I am glad that this Supreme Court ruling takes that option away from electors. Although I wasn't involved in the case, my actions and those of all the rogue electors brought this case before the Supreme Court, which brought about the ruling that is in line with what I wanted.

I was not trying to overrule the will of the voters in 2016. During Hawaii's Democratic primary, 70% of the voters chose Bernie Sanders. I had been elected by Berniecrats at the Hawaii Democratic Convention to vote for Bernie in the general election. So, my vote for Bernie in the Electoral College was in line with the actual will of Hawaii voters.

By the time I voted as an elector, Hillary had already lost. My voting for her would not have changed the results of the Electoral College decision. Not wanting to waste my vote, I voted for Bernie. First off, as Hillary's emails have proven, Hillary, the DNC, and corporate media had colluded to successfully steal the nomination from Bernie and us all. I did not believe I should approve this theft by voting for Hillary. Secondly, I believed that the millions of Berniecrats who had worked hard and sacrificed to get Bernie elected had earned at least one Electoral College vote. So, I gave it to them. It was the right thing to do.

Throughout my conversations with this assorted group of individuals of different political beliefs and priorities, we talked a great deal about dysfunction—whether the dysfunction lies in the Electoral College, party politics, or actual governance. "The system is broken," Robert Satiacum summarizes. "So, how are we actually going to get it to work? This Supreme Court case on faithless electors isn't going to automatically fix it."

In spite of his rogue faithless vote, Robert shared that he had been invited to attend a local Democratic Party meeting in the lead-up to the 2020 presidential election. Enthusiastic to be invited back into the group, he attended it. By the end, he found himself slightly depressed and viewed it as a waste of an afternoon. "This is the exact same chaos we saw in 2016: the same signs; the same slogans; the same robocalls. Come on! I know that we are better than this," he exclaims. "We need to find a grounded leader. As for me, I say Faith Spotted Eagle 2020."

August 1, 2020

Acknowledgments

I cannot begin the acknowledgments without first expressing my deep gratitude to the eight electors who trusted me enough to allow me to share their story. Throughout the course of writing this book, I have come to respect each and every one of them. Not only did each one dedicate hours upon hours to our phone interviews, their enthusiasm and support for my writing certainly kept me going during the days when I considered giving up on this book.

Over the years of thinking about this topic, I have read a number of works that certainly influenced how I approached the Electoral College. Besides Robert Alexander (whose research I have highlighted in this book), works by James Lucas, Josiah Peterson, James Michener, Roger MacBride, George Edwards, and Tara Ross were insightful. Additionally, I appreciated *Politico*'s Kyle Cheney and his careful reporting on the 2016 electors and the nascent Hamilton Electors movement, as well as materials published by the Federal Election Commission, including those by William Kimberling.

Getting this book off the ground would not have been possible without the encouragement of James McCrone and John Hillen for my self-publishing ambitions. I would like to thank my meticulous editor, Jaya Chatterjee, as well as Robert Alexander for reviewing many of the historical chapters for inaccuracies. Ryan Clark has also been a creative sounding board for me for over a decade. His infographics and designs helped make my book come to life in ways that words alone simply could not do.

On a personal note, I would like to thank my dear friend Tcybzhid Tcybikova, who believed in me and encouraged me to pursue this research at its earliest stages. I also want to thank the world's best neighbor, Maggie Jin, who let me use her home internet for research and interviews when I had internet problems. A significant portion of this book was written in Toyohashi, Japan, where I escaped much of the wrath of the coronavirus with my aunt-in-law, Wei Wang, her husband, Qiang Yao, and my cousin-in-law, Heyi Yao. I want to thank them for providing a perfect environment for writing, along with a seemingly endless supply of coffee, plum wine, and sashimi.

I want to thank my husband, Tian Ai, for his constant positivity, his belief that I could finish this book (even when I was only a couple dozen pages into it), and his insightful comments on my first draft. Last, but certainly not least, I would like to thank my parents, David and Catherine Conrad, for always believing in me. Without their encouragement, writing this book would have been impossible.

"Now faith is confidence in what we hope for and assurance about what we do not see." —Hebrews 11:1

About the Author

Emily Conrad attended Wofford College in her hometown of Spartanburg, South Carolina, where she graduated *summa cum laude* with a triple major in economics, German, and Spanish, and the distinction of Phi Beta Kappa. She completed a Master of Law in China Studies, focusing on international relations at Peking University in Beijing, China, where she was a Yenching Academy fellow. Emily enjoys reading about history and politics, singing and attending the opera, as well as playing classical piano. *The Faithless? The Untold Story of the Electoral College* is her first book.

Do you have a question about the Electoral College? Do you have your own elector story to share? If so, Emily Conrad wants to hear from you! Visit www.emilycconrad.com or connect via social media.

Facebook: @TheFaithlessBook
Instagram: emilycconrad
Twitter: emilycconrad